501

practical ways to

love

your

Grandparents

Roger,
Robin, &
Jacob
Sonnenberg

CPH
SAINT LOUIS

Copyright © 1999 Concordia Publishing House
3558 S. Jefferson Avenue, St. Louis, MO 63118-3968
Manufactured in the United States of America

Library of Congress Cataloging-in-Publication Data

Sonnenberg, Roger.
    501 ways to love your grandparents / Roger Sonnenberg.
        p.   cm.
    ISBN 0-570-05487-7
    1. Grandparents. I. Title. II. Title: Five hundred and one ways to love your grandparents. III. Title: Five hundred and one ways to love your grandparents.
HQ759.9.S67   1999
306.874'5—dc21   99-30820

 1 2 3 4 5 6 7 8 9 10   08 07 06 05 04 03 02 01 00 99

I have been reminded of your sincere faith, which first lived in your grandmother Lois and in your mother Eunice and, I am persuaded, now lives in you also. 2 Timothy 1:5

This book is dedicated in fond remembrance to two grandmothers and a father who greatly influenced us and are now enjoying the bliss of heaven:

Grandma Margaret Schriver

Nanny Hilda Ijames

Reinhart Sonnenberg

and in thanksgiving to the special grandparents who are now mentoring and loving our son, Jacob:

Bertha Sonnenberg

Jack and Joyce Ijames

Edna Werman, surrogate grandmother

Contents

Preface   9

Introduction   11

Love Them with Special Gifts   15

Love Them with "Grand" Tidbits of Truth   87

Love Them by Sharing Time   113

Love Them by Sharing Something Handmade   137

Love Them by Sharing Thoughts   167

Preface

One thing we learn from the Asian culture is the importance of paying respect to older people. In contrast, our culture is more focused on youth, often paying little or no respect to those who are older and wiser. Throughout Scripture God affirms the value of the aged: "Gray hair is a crown of splendor" (Proverbs 16:31). We write books on how to love our children and our children's children, but too often we forget that grandparents are also people who need to be respected, affirmed, and shown love.

We've come up with 501 suggested ways to *love* grandparents. This book is for all grandchildren—young and old. The introductory sections of the book are set off to be read only by older grandchildren and parents of younger grandchildren. Each suggestion is marked in one of three ways:

 Indicates the suggestion is for younger children

 Indicates the suggestion is for older children

 Indicates the suggestion is for both younger and older children

There are five main sections in the book that give suggestions on how to love your grandparents:

1. Love Them With Special Gifts
2. Love Them with "Grand" Tidbits of Truth
3. Love Them by Sharing Time
4. Love Them by Sharing Something Handmade
5. Love Them by Sharing Thoughts

Our prayer is that this book will help grandchildren of all ages remember not only that their grandparents are people too, but more important, they are God's people loved by Him and they need to be loved by us. Our hope is that these suggestions will help you better love your grandparents with your words and actions.

Jacob, Robin, and Roger Sonnenberg

Introduction

It was the phone call I knew would come someday … the one informing me something had happened to one of my parents.

"Roger, Dad had a heart attack," my sister said, crying. "We're so worried he's not going to make it …"

Plans for going home started going through my mind, but I knew I needed to wait to see how serious the heart attack actually was.

Several hours later it appeared Dad had stabilized. Less than eight hours later, however, came a phone call to come home. Dad had suffered a severe stroke, and the doctor felt the family should come quickly if we wanted to see him alive.

That night I took a red-eye flight from Los Angeles to Minneapolis, then on to Fargo. The trip from Fargo, North Dakota, to Detroit Lakes, Minnesota, seemed like an eternity. I didn't know if Dad had even made it through the night.

The intensity of the power that was lifting me, keeping me strong, was overwhelming. It was surely God answering the prayers of His people—those in my congregation and others. He was supporting me to do something I feared I would never be able to do: face the reality of the death of one of my parents. I kept asking, "What will I find?"

As I walked down the long hallway, I learned Dad was still alive. Ginny, my sister, saw me coming and, crying, came to hug me. We went immediately into the intensive care unit. I found my dad as I had never seen him before—helpless and incapacitated by a paralysis that had come so quickly, so suddenly!

I held back my tears as I kissed Mom and went to the hospital bed.

"Hi, Dad! It's Roger," I said as I awkwardly hugged him. Countless tubes and machines held him captive.

Then, almost instinctively, I retreated into being a pastor. I started talking to him as if I were talking to one of my parishioners! As I look back, I know why—it was to protect myself. I wanted to believe this really wasn't my father. I talked with him, but he could not respond. I held back my tears. I didn't want him to think I was there because he was dying. I wanted to encourage him, to assure him the stroke would not incapacitate him for life. I tried to tell him that, but not very well. I prayed with him, pleading that God would spare him.

"Stop it!" I finally said to myself. "This is the man you're named after! Your flesh and blood! Stop it! Stop long enough to be with him, to just hold his hand, to listen to him talk if he wants to … if he can …"

It took a while, but the severity of my father's condition became apparent. Other family members arrived. My nieces and nephews, their children, other relatives came to the bedside, all because they loved this man.

Over the next few days, I saw ministry differently—ministry to those I usually visited in the hospital, those who were with family members suffering from a stroke, heart attack, or cancer. Before, I was the one who ministered. Now

I was the one who needed the ministry!

Here lay a father who always had been strong, always had seemed indestructible, one who had never been in the hospital in his life. But now helpless, paralyzed, a different man. The family and I stood next to him, talking, hoping, praying.

As I left his bedside Friday afternoon, I prayed with him, cupped his face in my hands, kissed him on the forehead, and told him I loved him. Then I walked away, down the hall, refusing to turn or to look back or to see anyone walking by me. I wanted simply to go without anyone seeing the tears pouring down my cheeks. I was ready to return home to California. I didn't want to talk to anyone; I wanted to be alone.

I felt so helpless. I wanted to do more and I couldn't. I wanted to run back and reassure my mom that the paralysis would go away, but I couldn't lie. The doctor said it more than likely wouldn't. I wanted to run back and tell my sister and brothers I'd be there for them, and they wouldn't have to bear the burden alone, but I couldn't. It wouldn't be true!

I drove toward the darkening clouds of a summer storm. Lightning flashed in the distance, and it was almost as if God were scolding me. "O ye of little faith ..." The words of the pastor who had visited with us earlier in the afternoon echoed in my ears, "And God is faithful; He will not let you be tempted beyond what you can bear. But when you are tempted, He will also provide a way out so that you can stand up under it" (1 Corinthians 10:13).

A month and a half later I received another phone call. My brother's words were not welcome: "Roger, Dad passed away tonight." A wave of emotion went through me. My sister voiced my feelings, "Roger, he was supposed to get better."

I was glad my father was no longer paralyzed. I was sad that Robin, Jacob, and I had waited until this year to spend the first Thanksgiving since I graduated from the seminary with my family. It was too late now. There would be no Thanksgiving with Dad; he was gone. My son would not be able to ice fish with Grandpa—something he had never done. There would be no more visits in the garage, just Jacob and Grandpa, talking about the "monstrous fish" that Grandpa almost caught. There were tears of gladness, tears of regret. But always, during that sleepless night, there were arms—large arms—embracing me: God's arms. His arms conveyed forgiveness, brought healing, brought comfort.

When one is most helpless, most paralyzed with fear, one understands God's love more deeply. Like Peter, I had to ask, "Lord, to whom shall we go? You have the words ..." (John 6:68). No one but Jesus Christ could bring me any real comfort. "He who did not spare His own Son, but gave Him up for us all—how will He not also, along with Him, graciously give us all things?" (Romans 8:32).

It is my prayer that my father's death, the passing of my son's grandfather, might impress on you the urgency to love your parents and your grandparents with your words and actions before God takes them home. It is my prayer that God will give you the wisdom to know just the right time and place for some special word or act that will say, "I love you." It is my prayer that you will "make the most of every opportunity" (Ephesians 5:16) to love some very special people in your family—your parents and your grandparents.

Love Them with Special Gifts

D o you remember mission festivals? They were annual events that celebrated foreign mission work, usually held outside, often under the trees or in a tent. A potluck dinner and special activities followed. I remember especially the festivals held at St. Paul's in Vergas, Minnesota.

What made mission festivals so memorable? Was it the food? the fellowship? the missionaries who came as guest speakers? As wonderful as those things were, what made the festivals so memorable was what took place on the field behind the cemetery: a softball game. The older folks played the kids. There wasn't any choosing of teams; everyone got to play. Everyone was affirmed. No one said, "You get Roger!" There wasn't any teasing or taunting if you didn't hit the ball. In fact, the adults did everything in their power to help you get a hit!

I remember once at bat when I was 11. I swung, and the wooden bat cracked as it connected with a fast-moving softball. The ball flew high into the air, beyond the barbed wire fence that kept the Richters' cows from eating flowers off the graves. Everyone cheered for me, the one no one ever wanted on the team!

The softball game was more than a game. It was a prelude, a tiny glimpse of a sacred fellowship we will someday share in heaven. For a clumsy little boy, who was never chosen first on the school playground, the game was about grace—bountiful grace, wonderful grace. It was about acceptance, even if you were the worst player on the field.

There was a different attitude, a different spirit, in those church softball games. Could it have been because the tombstones surrounding the field echoed the silent reminder: *Hey, there's more to life than winning a softball game?* What does it profit a man to be the best player in town or to win the world championship yet lose his soul? (See Luke 9:25.)

Yes, I have fond memories of old-fashioned mission festivals—because of grace on a softball field. It was the grace of a loving God who sent His Son to die for the sins of the world and for my sins too. It was the grace I saw in others through the transforming power of the Holy Spirit. That same grace empowered me to be all I could be.

Empowerment doesn't come from the Law. It comes from the gift of grace—God's grace. We share this grace with others because of the grace given to us through Jesus Christ.

Grace is a gift! It is something you can give your grandparents. However, it is only one of many things you can give them. The gift might be your presence. It might be a packet of seeds. Giving something to someone is a way of saying I love you. Giving a gift to someone says, "I'm thinking of you" or "I remember you." The cost of the gift is not important. The thought is.

Everyone, including grandparents, needs to know they're needed. One way to encourage grandparents is to send herbs as monthly reminders of the contributions they make in your life. Local greenhouses often have live plants, even in the winter. Many of the herbs can also be grown from seeds. Send herbs with a message as follows.

Thyme

In the Middle Ages, thyme was given to knights before they went into battle because it was believed to increase courage. Give your grandparents this plant as a thank you for their many teachings and lessons that help you be courageous.

Sage

The word *sage* comes from the Latin word *salvere,* which means "to save." It was thought to be a "cure-all." Use this herb to thank your grandparents for the times they've taught you about Jesus, the cure-all for life and for death.

Rosemary

Rosemary is touted as the herb that increases memory. Hamlet said, "That's Rosemary, That's for remembrance; I pray you, love, remember." Send this herb to your grandparents after a special time when they have remembered you.

Garlic

This herb is also known as "Russian penicillin" because it was used successfully as a disinfectant and a treatment to prevent gangrene. Dr. Albert Schweitzer, a missionary in Africa, used it to treat a whole range of diseases. This herb is also pungent when added to food. You might want to tell your grandparents that, just as garlic adds a special flavor to food, they add a special flavor to your life.

Parsley

This herb purportedly relieves indigestion and helps clear congestion caused by coughs or colds. It also freshens one's breath. Remind your grandparents they are like a breath of fresh air in your life.

Peppermint

Studies have shown that peppermint relaxes the stomach muscles, preventing stomachaches and heartburn. Send this herb to your grandparents to remind them that just as peppermint helps with heartburn, they help make your heart healthier and happier when they visit or make time for you.

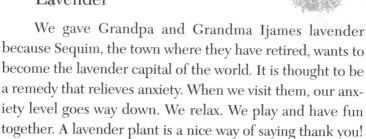

Lavender

We gave Grandpa and Grandma Ijames lavender because Sequim, the town where they have retired, wants to become the lavender capital of the world. It is thought to be a remedy that relieves anxiety. When we visit them, our anxiety level goes way down. We relax. We play and have fun together. A lavender plant is a nice way of saying thank you!

After an Extended Vacation

Bonding between grandparents and grandchildren takes place especially during extended vacations. However, as much as they enjoy this time with their grandchildren, it is also exhausting for them. We always tease our grandparents in Washington after an extended vacation with us, that they must sleep for days.

After an extended vacation, write Grandma and Grandpa a note with some special encouragement, such as:

"When God measures a man, He puts the tape around the heart instead of the head." I know God's tape was really stretched this last week as He measured your hearts. Thanks for giving so much of your love to your grandson the last few weeks. You're so special. Remember, "The LORD does not look at the things man looks at. Man looks at the outward appearance, but the LORD looks at the heart" (1 Samuel 16:7b). Be assured, your hearts look good not only to your grandson, but to us as well, and, more important, to God.

9 Remembering the Simpler Things

"The great man is he who does not lose his child's heart." — Mencius

In the movie *Jack*, the title character is a child who grows unusually fast, becoming a man in size by age 8. At first, he's the target of attack from children his own age; but, with time, they begin to love him as one of their own. At his senior graduation, his classmates vote him the one they would most like to emulate. One student summarized it like this, "He's the only adult who sees things through a child's eyes."

When I heard the line, I thought of my father. He always loved and enjoyed every aspect of life, almost as if he were seeing each day through a child's eyes. Each time I saw him interact with my son, I saw that same wonderful quality. He wasn't pretending to do the crazy things my son likes, he really liked doing them!

If your grandchildren have a "Jack-like" grandparent, why not thank him or her with a note or telephone call?

"Thanks, Mom, for being one of my son's best friends— one who doesn't just get dragged to the toy stores, but who actually enjoys going there herself; one who doesn't just pretend to laugh at silly cartoons, but who likes them as much as he does. Mom, you'll never be old to your grandson or to me. Thanks."

T-I-M-E Spells Love

Stitch a special sign for grandpa's office or simply do it with crayons or colored markers.

"A gentleman is a gentle man, like you, Grandpa!"

Thank God for Grandparents

Write a special prayer of thanks for your grandparents. Pray it, then send it to them, saying, "This is what I thanked God for today."

An Attitude Adjustment

Ask yourself:

1. Do I grow impatient and irritable toward a grandparent who isn't able to keep up with me as we walk through the mall?
2. Do I grow impatient and irritable toward a grandparent who can't hear as well as she used to and I feel I have to shout for her to hear me?
3. Do I get angry when my grandparent becomes incontinent in a public place?
4. Do I make fun of a grandparent because he can't drive like he used to?
5. Do I pay my grandparents the same respect I want them to pay me?

13

God's Masterplan in Life

A poet once wrote:

I believe in God's masterplan in lives.
He moves people in and out of people's lives.
And each leaves his mark on the other.
You find you are made of bits and pieces of
all who ever touched your life.
And you are more because of it,
And you would be less if they had not touched you.
Pray God that you accept the bits and pieces
in humility and wonder and never question,
And never regret.

—Author Unknown

Grandparents need to know their lives mattered to their grandchildren. They need to know our lives are better because of them, and would not be as good without them as grandparents. Tell your grandparents what has made you better because they are your grandparents. Give specific examples of how they've helped you "be more," such as: made you more compassionate toward animals, helped you have a sense of humor, provided the example of commitment in marriage.

Internal Jogging

Psychologists, psychiatrists, doctors, and counselors are advocating more laughter. Empirical evidence has shown that hospital patients who can relax and laugh get healthier faster. These same studies show that those who do not laugh are more susceptible to illness. Some call laughing "internal jogging." God's people can especially laugh. They can laugh at Satan because he's been defeated. They can laugh at death because death has been conquered. They can laugh and be glad because they are God's people, redeemed through the blood of Jesus Christ.

The next time you see your grandparents or talk to them on the telephone, tell a joke. Make them laugh. Help them live longer.

Humor is good for the soul.

A Secret Signal of Love

Decide on a secret signal that indicates you love one another. It might be pulling the ear three times or winking two times.

16 Laughter through a Gift

Send your grandparents a funny video (e.g., *Jungle to Jungle*), a funny book (e.g., one of Erma Bombeck's books), or a comedy tape (e.g., a recording of an "Amos and Andy" radio broadcast).

17 A Book

Send your grandparents the book *Life 101: Everything We Wish We Had Learned about Life in School—But Didn't* by Peter McWilliams. (Los Angeles, CA: Prelude Press, 1997).

18 Saved

Someone asked his friend, "Are you saved?"

The friend replied, "Yes. It happened on Good Friday and the hour was three o'clock in the afternoon."

Ask your grandparents to tell you when they were saved.

If they aren't, tell them about Jesus. Use these passages and others: Romans 3:10–12; John 3:16–17; Acts 16:31.

19 A Vinyl Placemat

Decorate a vinyl placemat with something special for your grandma, such as, "The best grandma in the world is sitting here."

20 Cross

On the tenth day of the first month the people went up from the Jordan and camped at Gilgal on the eastern border of Jericho. And Joshua set up at Gilgal the twelve stones they had taken out of the Jordan. He said to the Israelites, "In the future when your descendants ask their fathers, 'What do these stones mean?' tell them, 'Israel crossed the Jordan on the dry ground.' For the LORD your God dried up the Jordan before you until you had crossed over. The LORD your God did to the Jordan just what He had done to the Red Sea when He dried it up before us until we had crossed over. He did this so that all the peoples of the earth might know that the hand of the LORD is powerful and so that you might always fear the LORD your God …" Then the LORD said to Joshua, "Today I have rolled away the reproach of Egypt from you." So the place has been called Gilgal to this day. Joshua 4:19–24, 5:9*

The monument called Gilgal was a symbol of the victory God gave to the Israelites. The cross is a symbol of the victory we have received through the life, death, and resurrection of Jesus Christ.

> *When you were dead in your sins and in the uncircumcision of your sinful nature, God made you alive with Christ. He forgave us all our sins, having canceled the written code, with its regulations, that was against us and that stood opposed to us; He took it away, nailing it to the cross. And having disarmed the powers and authorities, He made a public spectacle of them, triumphing over them by the cross.* Colossians 2:13–15

Give your grandparents a cross for their home, or one for grandma to wear or for grandpa to carry in his pocket. When you give the cross, remind them of the story in Joshua 4:19–24, 5:9 and the assurance found in Colossians 2:13–15.

Hearts of Love

Cut paper hearts out of red construction paper and tie string or ribbon to them. Then tape them to your grandparents' kitchen doorway for them to walk through as a reminder of how much you love them.

How Old Am I?

Share the following poem with your grandparents this week.

How Old Am I?
Age is a quality of mind;
If you have left your dreams behind,
If hope is lost,
If you no longer look ahead,
If your ambitions are dead,
You are old.
But if from Life you take the best;
If in Life you keep the jest,
If Love you hold,
No matter how the years go by,
No matter how the birthdays fly,
You are not old.[1]

The Color of Love

Ask your grandparents which color they think best reflects love. Ask them to explain their answer. Then give them a small gift wrapped in paper the color they said best reflects love.

Show You Care

St. Paul rejoiced as people shared their concern for him: "I rejoice greatly in the Lord that at last you have renewed your concern for me" (Philippians 4:10).

Do something for your grandparents that shows you care, such as vacuuming their living room.

You've Made a Difference

Write a note to your grandparents thanking them for making a difference in your life.

Plant a Tree

Plant a tree on your grandpa's birthday and invite him to visit it with you at least once a year.

Drive into a Pathway of Love

Sometime when your grandparents are away, make a series of signs and put them along the driveway. Some ideas include

"Here come the grandest grandparents in the world!"

"Love to two super-duper people!"

"We're blessed with GRAND grandparents!"

A Special Tool

Grandpas are often very practical in nature, which means they appreciate practical gifts. Ask your grandpa what tool he needs for his garage or automobile, then buy it for him.

Kite Making and Flying

Ask grandma to help you make a kite. Directions for kite making can be found in books at your local library. Once you've made the kite, go out to an open field or the beach and fly it together.

"I Love You" in Pig Latin

Tell your grandparents you love them in pig Latin: "I-yay ov-lay ou-yay!"

A Surprise Package

Surprise your grandparents with a special package. How about sending them their favorite candy with a special note? Here's one Jacob sent to his grandpa when he was just a few years old:

Dear Grandpa,

I am sending your favorite candi. It is two sticks of red Lickerise. I took a bite out of each one so we could share the same candi. Like you always say, 'It's good to share!' Think of me when you eat it, Gramps.

I love you Lots.

Jacob.

"Don't Forget, I Love You!"

Enlarge a photograph of yourself. Write on the bottom of the picture, "Don't forget, I love you." Then hide the picture under your grandma's pillow.

A Picture and a Poem

When I was a child growing up on a farm in Minnesota, we used an old-fashioned pump to deliver well water. Before we pulled the handle, we had to prime the pump by pouring water into a pipe from above. When we visited the farm recently, we took a picture of the pump. We framed it, wrote a poem about it, and sent it to Grandma and Grandpa for Christmas. The poem read:

From the old rusted pipes
Flow sweet memories of our past.

Memories of hot summer days
And an old pump pouring forth
An endless supply of icy cold,
Thirst-quenching water—
Much like you, dear Mom and Dad,
Grandma and Grandpa.
Like the old farm pump,
You are a wellspring of love,
Which continues to overflow
From one generation to the next.
Thank you.

Why not take a picture of something memorable from the place your parents or grandparents grew up, frame it, and write a poem? The poem doesn't have to be anything great; your grandparents will love whatever you write.

How Many Ways Do I Love You?

Play a game with your grandparents, thinking of the many ways you love one another. You begin by saying, "I love you more than all the stars in the sky!" or "I love you more than all the bytes on my computer." Then ask them to tell you how they love you by beginning with the same words and completing it however they wish, "I love you more than ..."

A Half-birthday Card

Exactly six months before your grandpa's birthday, send him a birthday card and wish him the following: "Have a 'grand' wonderful half-birthday."

Love in a Balloon

Take a small slip of paper and write a message of love on it. Fold it up and slip it inside a deflated balloon. Then send it to your grandparents. Tell them you've sent a special message to them, but to read it, they will have to blow up the balloon and break it!

A Boat Trip

Rent a boat and give your grandparents a ride around a local lake.

Share Frozen Pops

Buy some ripe bananas, then peel and mash them into a smooth puree. Spoon the puree into small paper cups and freeze. Invite your grandparents over on a warm summer afternoon. Sit under a tree and serve them this yummy banana treat!

39 Feed the Birds

Collect pine cones. Buy a big jar of peanut butter, birdseed, and plastic storage bags. Tie string around each pine cone so it can be hung on a tree branch. Spread peanut butter on each one—lots of it. Then roll the cones in birdseed and carefully put them in the plasic bags. Place them in a short box, such as a shirt box. Wrap the box and send it to your grandparents. Tell them that, as yummy as the pine cones look, they're for the birds to eat, not for them! Ask them to report what they observe over the next few weeks after they have hung the pine cones outside.

40 Help with Yard Work

Offer to help your grandparents do yard work.

41 Scriptural Praying

We know that the Holy Spirit uses the Word as a way to give us God's grace, His love, His forgiveness. The Word has power. One way you can take advantage of this power is to use the words of Scripture as a prayer for others by inserting their names within the verse:

"Help _____ to remember that nothing is impossible with God" (Luke 1:37).

"Give _____ the wisdom that comes from heaven [which is] pure, peace-loving, considerate, submissive, full of mercy and good fruit, impartial and sincere" (James 3:17).

"Let _____ be strong in the Lord and in His mighty power" (Ephesians 6:10).

"May the Lord Jesus, that great Shepherd of the sheep, equip _____ with everything good for doing His will" (Hebrews 13:20b-21a).

"Help _____ to be anxious about nothing, but in everything, by prayer and petition, with thanksgiving, present his requests to God" (Philippians 4:6).

A Special Book

Purchase the book *Remember Me* by Margaret Wild (Morton Grove, IL: Albert Whitman & Company, 1995). Then sit down and read it with your grandma. It's a special book that talks about remembering things. Although we may forget some things as we grow older, it is hard to forget a loving grandchild.

Pray for One Another

Some interesting research proves empirically what Christians have known all along through faith: prayer works. For example, research in a large metropolitan hospital in California showed that patients who suffered major heart attacks and were being prayed for recovered much faster than those who were not prayed for.

Pray for your grandparents every day!

A Special Awards Banquet

Invite your grandparents to a special "Awards Banquet," which will take place during dinner at your house. When they arrive, they'll discover they were the only ones invited. During dinner, pass out buttons and ribbons honoring your guests ("Best Grandma" award, "Best Fisherman" award, etc.). Make sure your grandparents get all the awards.

The Lord's Prayer

The Lord's Prayer is a prayer for God's people because it affirms what God gives to a Christian.

Our Father in heaven,
hallowed be Your name,
Your kingdom come,
Your will be done on earth as it is in heaven,
Give us this day our daily bread,
Forgive us our debts, as we also have forgiven
our debtors.
And lead us not into temptation,
But deliver us from the evil one. Matthew 6:9–13

If your grandparents are Christians, you have great reason for joy. Celebrate this joy with this prayer:

"Thank You, God, for being our Father who is in heaven, … for being Grandpa and Grandma's heavenly Father.

"Thank You for making us 'hallowed' through the blood of Jesus Christ, … for making Grandpa and Grandma holy and blameless through the same blood.

"Thank You for giving us Your kingdom through faith in Jesus Christ … for giving Grandpa and Grandma the kingdom of heaven.

"Thank You that Your will is being done in our lives— our very salvation … for doing Your will in Grandpa and Grandma's hearts as well.

"Thank You for the assurance that You have and will

give us our daily bread … You will supply our every physical, emotional, and spiritual need … for giving Grandpa and Grandma their daily bread as well.

"Thank You for our forgiveness and the forgiveness we can give others because of Yours … for the forgiveness You have given Grandpa and Grandma over the years and continue to give them.

"Thank You for leading us away from the temptations of the world, the flesh, and the devil … for leading Grandpa and Grandma away from temptations that destroy faith, life, and hope.

"Thank You for delivering us from evil, especially the evil of sin, death, and the power of the devil … for delivering Grandpa and Grandma from the same evil.

"For we celebrate and rejoice that the kingdom of heaven and earth is Yours,

"All power is Yours,

And to Your glory and honor will all be done.

Amen, 'by the order and authority of God' we know it is true."

46 "I'm Nuts over You"

Fill a large jar with nuts. Tie a ribbon around the lid and attach a slip of paper to the end of the ribbon that reads, "I'm nuts over you!"

47 Photos

A must! Give your grandparents a school photo each year and ask them for a photo of themselves. Then be sure to post it on your family refrigerator door.

48 Sticky Notes

Buy sticky notes. Write a special love message on each sheet and then stick them everywhere in your grandparents' home (e.g., on the pillow, the front door).

49 Gift Certificates

Treat your grandparents to breakfast, lunch, or dinner by sending them gift certificates from a national fast-food chain such as McDonald's, Dairy Queen, or Denny's.

50 Make a Public Spectacle of Your Love

Use chalk to write a special message of affection to your grandparents on the sidewalk or driveway, such as, "Gramps, you're the best."

51 A Requested Hug

Put your ear up to your grandma's heart and say, "Your heart is telling me only one thing. You need a hug." Then hug her.

52 Return What You Borrowed

Have you borrowed something recently from your grandparents? If so, return it.

53 Bake Cookies

Instead of grandma sending you cookies, bake some and send them to her. They don't need to be anything fancy; chocolate-chip or sugar cookies are just fine.

54 Computer Lessons

Give your grandparents free computer lessons. Get a service provider (with software), such as America Online or Prodigy. Demonstrate computer functions that might prove useful for your grandparents.

If you convince them to get a computer or if they already have one, encourage them to get e-mail. It is one of the fastest and best ways to communicate with loved ones. Your mail will be received immediately and can be read at any time. Time zones won't make any difference. They can log on at any time and reply to the message.

An Eskimo Kiss

Give your grandpa an Eskimo kiss by rubbing your nose against his nose.

Music Appreciation

Find out what music your grandparents enjoyed years ago, purchase it, and listen to it. Then give the music to your grandparents as a gift, telling them what you did. Tell them what you liked about the music. Along with a copy of their favorite music, send them a copy of your favorite music. Ask your grandparents to listen to it and tell you what they think of it. Assure them they can be honest.

Dinner Out

Ask your grandparents which restaurant is their favorite. Take them there for a special evening out—with you picking up the bill.

58 Give Them Some Space

Baby-sitting can be tough, especially for older grandparents. The next time they baby-sit you, give them some space. Bring a book or video so your grandparents don't have to play with you, talk to you, or entertain you every minute.

59 Accept "No" Without a "Why?"

When your grandparents say no, don't argue with them. Accept it as the final word instead of asking, "But why?"

60 It's Show Time

Act out a play for your grandparents. Search the closet for costumes. Use background music. Present them with free admission tickets.

61 Foundation for Grandparenting

Put your grandparents' names and addresses on a sheet of paper and send it to:

Foundation for Grandparenting
Box 326
Cohasset, MA 02025

Ask for information on retreats available for grandparents and grandchildren.

62 An "Angel Kiss"

Give your grandpa an "angel kiss" by kissing his closed eyelids.

63 Scrub a Dub Dub

Wash grandma's car. Don't forget to clean the inside.

64 Sing a Song

Make a video tape of you and your grandparents singing verse three of "Amazing Grace":

Through many dangers, toils, and snares
I have already come.
His grace has brought me safe so far,
His grace will lead me home.

65 Write a Letter

Write a letter to your grandparents, even if they live next door to you! Tell them what they mean to you. And don't forget to say simply, "I love you."

Forgiveness

A pastor's son and his mother were shopping. The boy acted badly and the mother reprimanded him.

As the boy and mother were driving home, the boy knew his mother was angry. He asked, "Mom, Dad says that when God forgives us, He forgives us totally and completely. Is that true?"

"Oh yes," the mother said.

"And when He forgives us," the boy continued, "He buries our sins in the deepest part of the ocean. Is that right, Mom?"

"Oh yes, most certainly," his mom said.

The boy was quiet for a while, but finally said, "I asked God to forgive me for being bad while we were shopping." He paused for a moment. "But I suppose when I get home, we're going to go fishing for those sins again. Am I right, Mom?"

Thank God and your grandparents for the many times they've forgiven you and "hurl(ed) all (y)our iniquities into the depths of the sea" (Micah 7:19). You can do this through a special note or simply by talking to them about the reality and beauty of forgiveness.

#1 Grandma

Buy a special pendant or pin for your grandmother that says, "#1 Grandma."

Spontaneous Telephone Call

On the spur of the moment, phone your grandparents and say, "I just wanted to tell you I love you. In my book, you'll always be number 1!"

Popcorn and a Little Chat

Invite your grandparents over for popcorn and a little chat. Enjoy the popcorn with your grandparents—but not in front of the TV. Eat it where you and your grandparents can talk.

A Family Photograph

Arrange for a professional photographer to take a family picture. Tell your grandparents that you'd like to take them out for dinner (tell them to dress up), then drive them to the photographers' studio for the picture. Surprise them!

Color a Picture

Color a picture from a coloring book and send it to your grandparents. Ask them to post it on the refrigerator.

A Picture Puzzle

Turn a picture of your family into a puzzle at your local photo lab. Break it up and send it to your grandparents.

Clean Their House

Declare a work day and help your grandparents clean their home. Listen to music while you work. Be creative in your musical selections; for instance, you could purchase a cassette of Sousa's marches to play while you clean.

What Would Jesus Do?

Most religious bookstores carry special bracelets and necklaces that have the monogram: W W J D ? It stands for "What Would Jesus Do?" Purchase a piece of jewelry for your grandparents.

"Waiting for the Wind"

Give your grandparents the video *Waiting for the Wind* (St. Louis, MO: Family Films, Lutheran Hour Ministries, 1991).

A Special Prayer When Grandpa Is Sick

When your grandpa is sick, encourage him with the words of Psalm 91:14–16, inserting his name in the verse:

> "Because _____ loves me," says the LORD, "I will rescue _____; I will protect_____, for _____ acknowledges My name. _____ will call upon Me, and I will answer him; I will be with _____ in trouble, I will deliver _____ and honor him. With long life will I satisfy _____ and show him My salvation."

Dying for Praise

Often we wait until funeral services to praise people and celebrate their lives. Don't wait for your grandparents to die to praise them. Do it today.

Plan a Weekend Getaway

Surprise your grandparents by planning a special "Getaway Weekend" for them. Arrange for hotel accommodations and, if needed, provide transportation. Whatever it takes to make them to have a great weekend alone, do it. Tell them it's a "second honeymoon." When they give you one excuse after another for not being able to go, tell them you've taken care of their excuses. You'll feed the dog. You'll water the yard, etc.

Bake an Angel Food Cake

Bake an angel food cake and leave it at your grandparents' door with a little note: "Angel food cake for you because I think you're angelic!"

Greeting Cards and Stamps

Greeting cards, once inexpensive, are now almost as expensive as the gift you buy. Buy an assortment of them (i.e., birthday, grief, "thinking of you") for your grandma. Arrange them in file folders so she can easily find an appropriate card for any occasion. She'll appreciate not needing to run to the store for a card. To top it all off, give her a roll of postage stamps so she'll have everything she needs to remember family and friends at special times throughout the year.

A Special Coupon

Present your grandpa with a special coupon good for one free back rub or a shoe shine (or whatever "service" you want to give).

Prescription for Health

When your grandma is sick, get a large helium balloon and tie a can of chicken soup to the string.

Visit an Amusement Park

Why do we expect our grandparents to take us to the amusement park? Why don't you take your grandparents? You pay. Ask *them* which rides they'd like to try. Make sure they get all they want of cotton candy, soda, ice cream, etc. Make it their day! When you see them having fun, you'll have fun as well.

Breakfast in Bed

The next time you spend the night with your grandparents, tell them you'd like to bring them breakfast in bed. Get up early and fix breakfast, or ask your dad to drop by with something from McDonald's. Whatever you feed them, your grandparents will enjoy the attention and the care.

Meaningful Touch

When you see your grandparents, embrace them. Tell them how happy you are they are your grandparents.

Hugs

Spontaneously hug your grandparents.

Hold Hands

When you're in church with your grandparents, hold your grandma's hand while listening to the sermon.

Vacuum under the Furniture

Offer to vacuum those difficult areas of your grandparents' house, such as under the furniture.

Fortune Cookie Notes

Buy a bag of fortune cookies. Pull out the fortunes with a tweezer. Then cut up strips of paper and write your own notes of love on them, such as, "You're the grandest, greatest, most gracious grandparent in this grand world." Then insert the messages into the cookies and present them to your grandparents to open whenever they desire.

Candy Kisses

If you have long-distance grandparents, send them a bag of Hershey's Kisses. Tell them that these "kisses" will have to do until you see them again.

Attitude

A sign over General Douglas MacArthur's desk in Tokyo read: "Youth is not a time of life—it is a state of mind. You are as young as your faith, as old as your fear; as young as your hope, as old as your despair."[2]

Place this saying on a plaque for your grandparents. A unique way to do this is to take a weathered board about a foot long and paint the words on it.

To the Zoo

Take your grandparents to the zoo.

Freshly Squeezed Orange Juice

Make some freshly squeezed orange juice for your grandparents.

"Thinking of You" Card

Send your grandparents a "Thinking of You" card.

A Birdfeeder

Bring a birdfeeder for your grandparents and hang it outside near their living room or kitchen window so they can see the birds using it.

"I Love Lucy"

Rent some "I Love Lucy" episodes from your local video store and watch them with your grandparents.

Take Out the Garbage

Go over to your grandparents' house early one morning and, before the garbage collector comes, take their garbage out for them.

A Letter from a Magazine

Cut out words from an old magazine or newspaper to make up a special letter for your grandparents.

99
A Short Trip

Invite your grandparents to take a short trip with you via the bus, train, or ferry.

100
Polish Your Grandpa's Shoes

Polish your grandpa's shoes without being asked.

101
Eight Glasses of Water a Day

Encourage your grandparents to drink at least eight glasses of water a day.

102
In Your Prayers

Always include your grandparents in your prayers. Ask them if they have any special concerns they'd like you to pray for.

103
Donate a Book

Donate a special book to the local library in honor of your grandma's birthday.

Feelings

When you talk with your grandparents, share how you're feeling. When your grandparents talk with you about a special concern, ask how they feel. Once they share their feelings, verbally validate what they tell you about their feelings.

Read the Bible

Read the Bible with your grandparents.

Receive Gifts

One of the primary love languages Gary Chapman speaks of in his book *The Five Love Languages* (Chicago, IL: Northfield, 1992) is "receiving gifts." Resolve to speak this love language to your grandparents (e.g., buy them their favorite candy, give your grandma a bottle of her favorite perfume).

Acts of Service

Another of the love languages Gary Chapman speaks of in his book *The Five Love Languages* is "acts of service." Resolve to speak this love language to your grandparents (e.g., wash the dishes piled in the sink, scrub your grandma's kitchen floor).

108 Party Time

Plan a simple, fun party for your grandparents and their friends.

109 Value

Find a favorite saying that tells your grandparents how much you value them. Put the saying on a plaque, and present it to your grandparents. Tell them the saying describes one of the reasons you love them.

110 A Special Song

Prepare a special song and sing it to your grandparents. Ask them to sing one of their favorite songs as you listen attentively.

111 Certainty of Heaven

Tell your grandparents why you're certain you're going to heaven: because you believe that Jesus Christ lived a perfect life to fulfill the Law, died on the cross in your place, and rose from the dead to assure you that your sins have been paid in full.

Thanks Be to God

Thank God for your grandparents.

Assurance

If your parents have divorced, assure both sets of grandparents that you are, and will always be, part of their family.

Talk with Your Eyes

When you talk to your grandparents, look them in the eye.

A Kiss Adds Life

One study from Germany suggested that kissing adds to a person's life. Add to your grandparents' life by kissing them when you say good-bye.

"I" Messages as Opposed to "You" Messages

Pledge to speak more "I" messages than "You" messages with your grandparents. ("You" messages can make the other person defensive. "I" messages often take the sting out of the statement.)

Something They Would Never Buy for Themselves

Bring a gift for your grandparents that they would never buy for themselves (e.g., some special dessert).

When Grandpa or Grandma Lives Alone

Arrange to have someone from the church check on your grandpa or grandma as often as you think is necessary (i.e., daily or weekly).

Light the Stairway

Many accidents occur because of poorly lighted stairways. Make sure your grandparents have working lightswitches at the top and the bottom of the stairs.

A Butterfly Kiss

The next time you see your grandpa give him a "butterfly kiss." It's done by fluttering your eyelashes on his cheek.

A Flashlight in Every Room

Make sure there is a working flashlight in every room of your grandparents' home.

First-Aid Kit

Purchase a first-aid kit for your grandparents. Make sure it is updated yearly.

Emergency Telephone Numbers

Make a list of emergency telephone numbers on cards that are large enough so the numbers can be seen and small enough so they can be easily posted near every telephone in your grandparents' home.

Electric Blanket

Make sure your grandparents' electric blanket is in good working order. If not, buy a new one for them.

Telephones Aplenty

Make sure there are telephones in all the main rooms, especially the kitchen, bedroom, and bathroom in your grandparents' home. If the telephones are ones you can program, program the emergency numbers into the phones for them.

A Tea Party

Plan a tea party with your grandma in the garden or on the lawn.

Nonskid Decals and Rubber Mats

Buy nonskid decals and rubber mats for your grandparents' shower and tub.

Grab Bars and Handrails

Install grab bars and handrails next to the toilet, the tub, and the shower.

Plan for the Snowstorm

If you live far away from your grandparents and cannot help them shovel the snow from their sidewalks and driveway, make arrangements for a neighbor or someone else to clear the snow. Tell your grandparents that as an early Christmas present or simply as a gesture of love, you've made arrangements for someone to shovel their snow and that you don't want them doing it.

Light on the Porch

Make sure all the porch lights on your grandparents' house are in good working condition.

Check the Extension Cords

Check the following for your grandparents:

1. All electric cords are in good working condition.
2. All electric cords are tucked away to prevent anyone from tripping on them.
3. Cords and outlets are not overloaded.

Smoke and Carbon Monoxide Detection

Make sure your grandparents' house has working smoke and carbon monoxide detectors. If not, purchase some and install them.

Check for Holes

Go through your grandparents' home and check to see if there are any holes or snags in the carpet. If so, get them fixed.

"Please Don't Climb on the Ladder"

Many grandparents insist on climbing ladders to clean windows, gutters, etc. Purchase easy-reach, long-handled sponges and dusters for them so they don't have to get on a ladder.

Check the Stairs Again and Again

Always check the stairs in your grandparents' home to see if there are any items stored on the steps that could cause them to fall. If so, remove them and tell your grandparents where you've put these items. Then, next week, check again … and again the next week.

Install a Peephole and Deadbolt Locks

Install a peephole and deadbolt locks on all the entry doors in your grandparents' house.

Safety Tip Review

Review with your grandparents some important safety tips such as:

1. Don't keep large amounts of cash in the house.
2. Don't open the door to strangers.

3. Draw blinds and shades at night.
4. Leave a light and a radio on while away from home.
5. Don't hide keys around the front door (i.e., under a mat).
6. Keep all bushes trimmed around the front door.
7. Suspend the newspaper and ask the post office to hold your mail while on an extended vacation.

Monthly Checks Deposited

Assist them in having their monthly checks deposited directly into their bank account.

PAL—"Phone Alert League"

Some communities provide a service called PAL—"Phone Alert League." It is a special service for anyone living alone. It is set up so at the same time each day the person checks in via the telephone. If the service does not hear from the individual, someone is sent to the person's residence. Find out if your grandparents' town has this service.

"Carrier Alert"

Sign your grandparents up for "Carrier Alert" through the postal service. A special sticker is placed on the mailbox. If mail accumulates, the postal worker is required to call the number on the sticker or the number left at the post office.

Home Safety Guide

Get a copy of the "Home Safety Guide" (free) from the AAA Motor Club office, and review it with your grandparents.

Life Savers

Send your grandparents a package of Life Savers with a note that says, "You're real Life Savers."

When Your Grandma Hurts

When your grandma is hurting, send her a bandage and write "I love you" on it.

Introduce Your Friends

If you have long-distance grandparents who don't get to meet your friends, introduce your friends to them via audio-tape (or videotape). The next time you have your best friends over, ask them to say a little about themselves on an audio-cassette tape. Have them introduce themselves and tell about their families. What do they like? What do you do when you all get together? Tell them you're asking them to do this because you'd like your grandparents to get to know them. Then send the tape to your grandparents. Why not ask your grandparents to do the same with their friends so you can get to know them as well?

Learn CPR

Take a CPR class (cardiopulmonary resuscitation). You can find these classes by checking the yellow pages under "First-aid Instruction," or by contacting your local branch of the Red Cross.

Legal Advice

If your grandparents have limited income and need legal advice, contact your local area council on aging, the AARP (American Association of Retired Persons), or the district attorney's office.

Web Sites

If your grandparents have a computer, or if you do, share with them the following Web sites:

- American Association of Retired Persons (AARP)—http://www.aarp.org

- American Bar Association—http://www.abanet.org

- American Medical Association—http://www.ama-assn.org

- Elderhostel—http://www.elderhostel.org

- Senior Net—http://www.senior.com

148 Help with Medication

The FDA (Food and Drug Administration) discovered that people 70 years and older fill an average of 13 prescriptions per year. Find out what these prescriptions are and whether a combination of any of them could be harmful (most pharmacists should be able to help you). If a grandparent is neglectful or forgetful, help him remember how to take his medication through easy charts or special containers that can be purchased through the pharmacy.

149 Attend a Health Fair

Find out when the local hospital or a health care group is having a free health fair. Invite your grandparents to attend with you. Most of these fairs offer free cholesterol and blood pressure testing.

Love Them Enough to Say "Let's Think This Through"

Some studies show that people age 85 and older have more serious injury and fatal automobile accidents than teenagers. If your grandparents are hazardous behind the wheel, take whatever steps you need to protect them and others.

1. Get help from his doctor to support you in encouraging him not to drive anymore.
2. Encourage her not to drive at night or during bad weather.
3. Encourage him to drive with the radio turned off.
4. Suggest alternative means of transportation.
5. Offer to drive for her as often as you can, or hire someone from her church.

Service Their Car

Make sure your grandparents' car is in good working condition. Check the brakes, the defogger, the battery, windshield wipers, etc.

A Cushion for Driving

If your grandma has trouble seeing clearly over the dashboard when driving, buy her a cushion. There are cushions made especially to raise a person up on the seat. (Pillows slip and can actually deter a person's driving ability.)

If Disabled

If your grandpa is disabled and lives alone, make sure his home is user-friendly. Helpful hints are available through a free booklet entitled, *Home Safe Home: How to Prevent Falls in the Home* from The American Association for Retired Persons (AARP) (Call 1-800–424–3410).

A Ride in the Country

If your grandparents don't get out much because of their health, take them for a ride in the country.

"Armchair Fitness"

If your grandparents are not in very good health but would like to exercise, ask a doctor or fitness expert to recommend an exercise video for seniors.

A Driver Refresher Course

Encourage your grandparents to take a driver refresher course to get a lower insurance premium (in most states), or for whatever other reason you think might be helpful. Such courses are available through the AARP (1–800–424–3410) or The National Safety Council (1–800–621–6244).

Install a Lazy Susan

Check to see if there are any hard-to-get-into kitchen cabinets in your grandparents' home. If so, install a lazy susan so they have easy access to every item.

A Tape of Your Recital or Baseball Game

If you have long-distance grandparents who can't be at your piano recital or baseball game, video tape the event and send it to them.

"You're Great"

Make a homemade card for your grandparents with the following letters and numbers somewhere on the card: U R G R 8 !

Brain Teasers

Ask your grandparent:

1. Which is heavier, a pound of rocks or a pound of feathers?
(Answer: Both weigh the same—a pound.)

2. What word do you see in the following arrangement of letters?

W
O
R
G

(Answer: Grow Up)

3. What phrase do you see in the following arrangement of letters?

SHAME
YOU

(Answer: Shame on you)

A Handcart

If your grandparents walk to nearby stores for merchandise, buy them a handcart to carry their purchases.

A Bag of Rock Salt or Sand

If your grandparents live where they get snow and ice, buy them a bag of rock salt or sand so they can toss it on their icy steps.

Pamper Them

If your grandma lives alone or is in an assisted care facility, pamper her by washing and combing her hair or giving her a back or neck massage. (If she's receiving nursing care, make sure you check with the nurses first.)

Make Conversation Easier

If your grandpa has trouble hearing, sit or stand three feet in front of him when talking to him. Don't shout. Look him in the eye and speak clearly. Don't talk down to him.

"Coulda," "Shoulda," and "Woulda"

Too many people get stuck on "if only," or "coulda," "shoulda," and "woulda." Such thinking never changes things. If your grandparents have become stuck in this way of thinking, encourage them to look ahead and see what is and what can be.

Insist She Be Checked

Love is sometimes tough. One in every nine women who live to age 85 will develop some form of breast cancer. Encourage your grandma to have a yearly mammogram.

Insist on a PSA Test

Some studies show that as many as 30 to 40 percent of all men over 50 may have prostate cancer. The rate jumps to 60 to 70 percent of men over the age of 75. Encourage your grandpa to have a yearly PSA test (prostate-specific-antigen blood level test).

A Three-dimensional Album

Purchase and give to your grandma the album entitled, *Grandmother's Album*, a keepsake for sharing pictures and thoughts (New York, NY: Penguin Studio, 1992). It is filled with great questions to record memories and provides little pockets for photographs, etc.

A Grandmother Remembrance Book

Present your grandma with a copy of *Grandmother Remembers* by Judith Levy (New York, NY: Sewart, Taburi &

Chang Publishers, 1983). It contains pockets for photographs, newspaper clippings, etc., as well as plenty of space for recording written memories.

A Letter Picture

Write a letter and draw a picture at the same time to your grandparents. The letter-picture might look like any of the following ideas.

A Lemon Letter

Write a letter to your grandparents using lemon juice (fresh or bottled). It is invisible until you put heat to it. Use a paintbrush to write your message on a plain sheet of white paper. Send it to your grandparents and tell them the special message is just for them. Tell them it can only be read by turning on a bright light and holding the paper next to the light bulb. As the paper heats up, they should be able to read your message easily.

A Letter on a Roll

Write a letter to your grandparents using a roll of cash-register or adding-machine paper. Keep writing on the paper until you're finished, roll the paper back up, and put a rubber band around it to keep it together. Then send it to your grandparents. They'll enjoy the creative way you've chosen to communicate with them.

A Grandfather Remembrance Book

Present your grandpa with a copy of *Grandfather Remembers* by Judith Levy (New York, NY: HarperCollins Publishers, 1991).

"14,000 Things to Be Happy About"

Purchase a copy of *14,000 Things to Be Happy About* (New York, NY: Workman Publishing, 1990) for your grandparents. Ask them to underline things in the book they are happy about. Then ask them to show you what they've underlined.

175 A Stuffed Animal

When your grandma is feeling depressed, buy her a soft stuffed animal.

176 Special Greetings

Send your grandpa special notes corresponding to his age. For example, if your grandpa is celebrating his 69th birthday, send him some special greeting each day for 69 days before his birthday.

177 A Bouquet of Wildflowers

Pick a bouquet of wildflowers for your grandma.

178 When He Is Feeling Sick

The next time your grandpa is feeling sick, take him some soft tissues and some magazines to read.

If in the Convalescent Hospital

If your grandma is in a convalescent hospital or retirement home, ask the nurses or the person in charge if you can bring your pet (i.e., rabbit, dog, cat) to visit her. Research has shown that animals can cheer those in retirement and convalescent homes.

A Clip-on Book Light

Give your grandparents a clip-on book light for night reading.

A New Magazine Subscription

Send your grandparents a new magazine subscription.

A Limousine Ride and Dinner

Arrange for a limousine to pick up you and your grandparents for a special dinner out.

An Old Puzzle

Write a special love letter to your grandparents on the back of an old puzzle. Give it to them in pieces.

A Love Note in the Personals

Write a special message of love to your grandparents and place it in the personals of their local paper.

Clean the Inside of the Car

Clean the inside of your grandparents' car. Leave a love note on the dashboard.

The Greatest Book

Ask your grandpa what is the greatest book (other than the Bible) he has ever read. If possible, buy a copy of the book and present it to him.

One Family Photo

Ask your grandparents if they had only one family photo to keep, which one would it be. Once they've told you, secretly borrow it, then have it enlarged and nicely framed.

A Special Offering

Ask your grandparents if there is a special group or organization they would like memorials given to upon their deaths. Once they've told you, give an offering in their name, rejoicing that you still have them with you. You don't want to wait until they're dead to do something in appreciation for their love.

What Attracted Grandpa to Grandma?

Ask your grandpa what qualities and personality traits he found most attractive about your grandma. Put these qualities down on paper under the caption:

"Love to a 'Grand' Ma from Her Grandchildren as Seen by Grandpa a Few Years Ago."

I fell in love with her because … (put down all the things your grandpa shared with you).

What Attracted Grandma to Grandpa?

Ask your grandma what qualities and personality traits she found most attractive about your grandpa. Put these qualities down on paper under the caption:

"Love to a 'Grand' Pa from His Grandchildren as Seen by Grandma a Few Years Ago."

I fell in love with him because … (put down all the things your grandma shared with you).

Give Grandma a Manicure

Give grandma a manicure and paint her nails.

Open the Door

Open the door for your grandparents.

Play a Game of Checkers

Play a game of checkers with grandpa.

People Watching

Invite your grandparents to go to the park with you to do nothing but sit on a bench and watch people.

Barefooted

Invite your grandparents to go barefoot with you after it has rained. Walk through the mud puddles and swish your toes in the mud.

Play a Game

Play a board game with your grandparents (e.g., Pictionary, Monopoly).

Flowers

Cut some fresh flowers from your garden, and put them by your grandma's bedside.

Homemade Get-well Cards

If your grandpa is ill, ask your friends from school, the neighborhood, or Sunday school to make cards with pictures on them to cheer him up.

Soft Pajamas

If your grandma is ill, buy her a pair of soft pajamas or a soft nightgown. Soft pajamas have a way of offering a special hug.

Share a Favorite Comic Strip

Cut out your favorite comic strip, and send it to your grandparents.

Confide a Secret

Confide your deepest, darkest secret to your grandpa.

Commemorate with a Tree

Commemorate your grandma's birthday by planting a tree.

Braid Her Hair

Sit outside under a tree and braid your grandma's hair.

Kiss in Public

Kiss your grandparents in a public place, and pretend no one is looking (but secretly hope someone is).

"I Need Your Help!"

Think of something you need help with, then call your grandparents and say, "I need your help ..."

Splash It on You and Grandpa

Buy your grandpa some very special cologne and splash it on him and on yourself as well. Tell him the smell joins you as "one."

Splash it on You and Grandma

Buy some special perfume for your grandma and splash it on both of you. Tell her the smell joins you as "one."

Squish, Squish

The next time you're with your grandparents at the ocean or a nearby lake, take off your shoes and squish wet sand or mud between your toes. Describe the feeling to one another.

A Whisper in the Ear

The next time the whole family is talking together about unimportant things, go over to your grandpa and whisper into his ear, "I love you."

Compliment and Excuse

The next time you eat at your grandparents' home, be sure to compliment the cook on the food. Also be sure to ask permission to be excused before leaving the table.

Be on Time

The next time you're at your grandparents' home and they call you for dinner or lunch, come immediately. If you don't come when asked, you're telling them that they're not important.

No Snooping

When you're at your grandparents' home, don't open drawers or desks without asking permission. Don't look at their personal mail. Remember, snooping is impolite.

Write an Enormous Letter

The next time you feel something is really important, write your grandparents a letter that shows the importance of the matter. Get some large white butcher paper, a large marking pen, and write the letter. Be prepared; you'll need a large envelope too.

Secret Notes in Secret Places

Write secret love notes to your grandparents and hide them around their home (e.g., under the pillow).

A Long-stemmed Rose

Get a long-stemmed rose, put it in a slender vase, and present it to your grandma.

A Bouquet of Balloons

Buy a bouquet of balloons and present it to your grandparents for no reason other than to say "I love you."

A Garland Wreath

Buy garland or take some ivy and weave it into a laurel wreath for the head. Present it to your grandparents, and tell them they deserve such a wreath to wear as a crown for being grandparents who are the best in every way!

Chocolate-covered Strawberries

During strawberry season, buy big juicy red strawberries, dip them in melted chocolate, and present them to your grandparents.

A Love Letter

Give your grandparents a sheet of stationery and a pen and ask them to write themselves a special love letter.

A Giant Cookie

Make a giant cookie, then take a tube of icing and inscribe it with a special message to your grandparents. After giving it to them, tell them to be sure to eat it with milk.

A Special Picture

Give each grandparent a special picture of you for his or her wallet or purse.

A Special Song

On your grandparents' wedding anniversary, call the local radio station and dedicate a special song to them.

A Message of Love in the Snow

Stamp out the words "I love you" in the snow in front of your grandparents' home.

A Special Calendar

Make a special calendar for your grandparents, and record all the special events of your family (i.e., birthdays, anniversaries).

For Traveling

As a gift for a long trip, buy your grandparents a neck pillow.

Love Them with "Grand" Tidbits of Truth

In their lifetime, grandparents share countless "grand" truths with their children and grandchildren. These truths helped us become who we are. They shaped our attitudes. They guided our consciences. They helped us see the bigger picture.

These truths include everything from passages of Scripture to bits of homespun wisdom. Often they are passed from one generation to the next. We make a mistake, however, when we think these truths can only be passed down from the top—from the older to the younger. Jesus said, "Let the little children come to Me, and do not hinder them, for the kingdom of God belongs to such as these. I tell you the truth, anyone who will not receive the kingdom of God like a little child will never enter it" (Mark 10:14–15). Jesus was indignant that anyone should think children were not important. He was saying we can learn from them. In their receptivity and dependence, children represent the characteristics of those who are members of God's kingdom.

There's a saying, "It takes a village to raise a child." It could be rephrased to say, "It takes a child to raise a village." The following example proves my point.

Two-and-half-year-old Jacob was excited when we told him we were going to the Los Angeles County Fair. We told him he would see cows like he saw during the summer on Papa Sonnenberg's farm. He could ride a pony and have some "yummies."

Upon arriving at the fair, however, Jacob spotted a train. From that time on, we heard one plea only, "Choo-choo train, Daddy ... Choo-choo train, Mommy."

The first ride was great. Jacob was alone, strapped into one of the open-air passenger cars. With each circle, he would put on a radiant smile and wave, almost like he was in the movies, obediently following the director's cues.

We told him he could go one more time, and he was strapped into the same passenger car. But this time two other children, both seemingly older than Jacob, were strapped alongside him. One of the children obviously did not want to be on the train. As the train started its journey once again, tears began to cascade down the boy's cheeks as he pleaded for release.

The first time around, Jacob did not wave as he had before. He only looked at the crying boy. The second time around, I feared he might start to cry himself. But the third time around, his actions brought tears to my eyes. He put his arm around the little boy, laid his head on his shoulder, and tried as best as he could to comfort him.

For a moment, it seemed to me that the cacophonous carnival calliope chimed out a new chord, a sound from Handel's Messiah, "Comfort ye My people, comfort ye, comfort ye My people, saith your God ..."

In an earthly, warm, wonderful way, Jacob reminded us of a wonderful truth. He became a picture for us of our heavenly Father, who puts His arms around us, invites us to lay our heads on His shoulder, and comforts us. Through the giving of His only begotten Son, He assures us: "Though your sins are like scarlet, they shall be as white as snow; though they are red as crimson, they shall be like wool" (Isaiah 1:18b).

As children and grandchildren, never forget that you can and must share with your parents and grandparents tidbits of truth that will help them on their journey in life. After all, grandparents are people too. They need encouragement. They need comfort. They need to see the bigger picture. Select one or two appropriate tidbits to share with your grandparents in the next week and see what happens.

From One Generation to the Next

Share the following truth with your grandparents:

"And he shall turn the heart of the fathers to the children, and the heart of the children to their fathers ..." Malachi 4:6.

Ask your grandparents which values they received from a previous generation and which ones they have tried to pass on to their children and grandchildren.

What Do You Think?

Ask your grandparents what they think about the following statement:

"To live is the rarest thing in the world. Most people exist, that is all." (Oscar Wilde)

When They Need to Know They're Loved

Share this wonderful truth with your grandparents:

How great is the love the Father has lavished on us, that we should be called children of God! 1 John 3:1

A Tidbit of Hope

Share the following tidbit of hope with your grandparents this week:

May the God of hope fill you with all joy and peace as you trust in Him, so that you may overflow with hope by the power of the Holy Spirit. Romans 15:13

To Commend a Cheerful Countenance

Share the following tidbit with your grandparents:
A *cheerful heart is good medicine.* Proverbs 17:22

A Tidbit about Newness

Pablo Casals, world-renowned cellist, said on his 93rd birthday, "Every day I am reborn, every day is a new lifetime for me."

Challenge your grandparents to make this their motto.

When Things Don't Seem Logical

Share with your grandparents this passage from Hebrews 11:1:

Faith is being sure of what we hope for and certain of what we do not see.

A Reminder That He Is Always Faithful

Remind your grandparents of 2 Timothy 2:13:

If we are faithless, He will remain faithful.

God Is …

Ask your grandparents what they think of God. Remind them of 1 John 4:16b:

God is love.

Share a Truth about Time

Age makes no difference. Remind your grandparents of the following wisdom from Scripture:

"As long as it is day, we must do the work of Him who sent Me. Night is coming, when no one can work." John 9:4

Saying No

Remind your grandparents that sometimes it's okay to say no. They can say no to baby-sitting. It's okay to not bail a son or daughter out of their financial troubles.

237

Always Growing

Share the following verse with your grandparents, reminding them they are still becoming what the Lord wants them to be:

Not that I have already attained all this, or have already been made perfect, but I press on to take hold of that for which Christ Jesus took hold of me. Philippians 3:12

238

Future Plans

Share with your grandparents the following promise:

"I know the plans I have for you, _____ (insert the names of your grandparents)," declares the LORD, "plans to prosper you and not to harm you, plans to give you hope and a future." Jeremiah 29:11

239

Who Are You and to Whom Do You Belong?

Remind your grandparents who they are and to Whom they belong through their faith in Jesus Christ by sharing this verse:

But you are a chosen people, a royal priesthood, a holy nation, a people belonging to God, that you may declare the praises of Him who called you out of darkness into His wonderful light. Once you were not a people, but now you are the people of God; once you had not received mercy, but now you have received mercy. 1 Peter 2:9–10

When They Feel Discouraged

Share the following Bible verse with your grandparents when they're feeling discouraged:

I can do all things through Christ who strengthens me. Philippians 4:13

One Hundred Years from Now

Remind your grandparents that one hundred years from now they won't be here and, more than likely, you won't be either. So why allow "small stuff" to keep us from enjoying "bigger and more important stuff"?

A Reason for Rejoicing

Remind your grandparents how thankful you are that you can rejoice "always" because you're "in the Lord." He will never fail you. Share the following Bible verse with them:

Rejoice in the Lord always. I will say it again; rejoice! Philippians 4:4

God Hears Our Prayers

Remind your grandparents that the Holy Spirit works through our prayers, even when we don't know what to pray:

In the same way, the Spirit helps us in our weakness. We do not know what we ought to pray for, but the Spirit Himself intercedes for us with groans that words cannot express. And He who searches our hearts knows the mind of the Spirit, because the Spirit intercedes for the saints in accordance with God's will. Romans 8:26–27

The Older the Better

Michelangelo once said, "The more the marble wastes, the more the statute grows." Remind your grandparents that though they may not be able to walk as well as they used to or see as far as they would like to, through the power of the Holy Spirit, they become more beautiful—more Christlike!

Rejoice over Your Salvation

Share the following Bible verse with your grandparents for no reason other than to rejoice together in your justification through Jesus Christ:

Since we have been justified through faith, we have peace with God through our Lord Jesus Christ. Romans 5:1

A Tidbit of Encouragement

If your grandparents are young at heart, remind them of the saying:

"To be 70 years young is sometimes far more cheerful and hopeful than to be 40 years old."

A Tidbit about Old Age

If your grandparents are always telling you that it's terrible to grow old, remind them: "The best thing about old age is that a person only has to go through it once."

A Tidbit about Worry

The next time your grandparents seem worried about something, remind them of God's promise in Matthew 6:25–26:

Therefore I tell you, do not worry about your life, what you will eat or drink; or about your body, what you will wear. Is not life more important than food, and the body more important than clothes? Look at the birds of the air; they do not sow or reap or store away in barns, and yet your heavenly Father feeds them. Are you not much more valuable than they?

A Tidbit of Advice on Work

If your grandparents are active, encourage them to stay active. Tell them, "It is better to wear out than to rust out."

Words That Build Up!

After talking with your grandparents, analyze the words you have spoken with the advice:

Finally, brothers, whatever is true, whatever is noble, whatever is right, whatever is pure, whatever is lovely, whatever is admirable—if anything is excellent or praiseworthy— think about such things. Philippians 4:8

Some Pleasant Words

Say something nice to your grandparents, reminding yourself of the words of Solomon:

Pleasant words are a honeycomb, sweet to the soul and healing of the bones. Proverbs 16:24

An Ideal Wife

Booth Tarkington once said, "An ideal wife is any woman who has an ideal husband." Ask your grandpa what he thinks made your grandma the ideal wife for him.

A Blessing for Them

Jot a note to your grandparents and share the following blessing with them:

The Lord Himself goes before you and will be with you; He will never leave you nor forsake you. Do not be afraid; do not be discouraged. Deuteronomy 31:8

No Reason for Fear

Remind your grandparents of God's promise of love for His people:

What, then, shall we say in response to this? If God is for us, who can be against us? He who did not spare His own Son, but gave Him up for us all—how will He not also, along with Him, graciously give us all things? Romans 8:31–32

No Condemnation

Share the following Scripture passage with your grandparents to remind them that no one can bring any condemnation against those whom God has chosen:

Who will bring any charge against those whom God has chosen? It is God who justifies. Who is he that condemns? Christ Jesus, who died—more than that, who was raised to life—is at the right hand of God and is also interceding for us. Romans 8:33–34

Assurance of God's Tremendous Love

Rejoice with your grandparents over God's tremendous love by sharing with them these words of Scripture:

Who shall separate us from the love of Christ? Shall trouble or hardship or persecution or famine or nakedness or danger or sword? ... No, in all these things we are more than conquerors through Him who loved us. For I am convinced that neither death nor life, neither angels nor demons, neither the present nor the future, nor any powers, neither height nor depth, nor anything else in all creation, will be able to separate us from the love of God that is in Christ Jesus our Lord. Romans 8:35, 37–39

The Most Loved Psalm

Memorize the following Psalm and say it to your grandparents:

The LORD is my shepherd; I shall not want. He maketh me to lie down in green pastures: He leadeth me beside the still waters. He restoreth my soul: He leadeth me in the paths of righteousness for His name's sake. Yea, though I walk through the valley of the shadow of death, I will fear no evil: for Thou art with me; Thy rod and Thy staff they comfort me. Thou preparest a table before me in the presence of mine enemies: Thou anointest my head with oil; my cup runneth over. Surely goodness and mercy shall follow me all the days of my life: and I will dwell in the house of the Lord for ever. Psalm 23 (KJV)

When Worried

If your grandparents are concerned about finances, remind them of God's promise:

God will meet all your needs according to His glorious riches in Christ Jesus. Philippians 4:19

For Those Who "Hope in the Lord"

Remind your grandparents of the wonderful promise given to all who "hope" in God:

But those who hope in the LORD will renew their strength. They will soar on wings like eagles; they will run and not grow weary, they will walk and not be faint. Isaiah 40:31

A Promise of Peace

Remind your grandparents of God's promise of strength and peace:

The LORD gives strength to His people; the LORD blesses His people with peace. Psalm 29:11

A God Who Never Forsakes His Own

Remind your grandparents that God never abandons His own:

For this God is our God for ever and ever; He will be our guide even to the end. Psalm 48:14

Someone to Go To

Rejoice with your grandparents that as Christians you have Jesus' promise:

Come to Me, all you who are weary and burdened, and I will give you rest. Take My yoke upon you and learn from Me, for I am gentle and humble in heart, and you will find rest for your souls. Matthew 11:28–29

A Special Promise to Older People

Sometimes people, as they mature in age, think no one cares. Remind them God does:

Even to your old age and gray hairs I am He, I am He who will sustain you. I have made you and I will carry you; I will sustain you and I will rescue you. Isaiah 46:4

After a Spouse Dies

God does not forget those who are left behind after the death of a spouse. When a grandparent loses his or her spouse, offer these words:

The LORD watches over the alien and sustains the fatherless and the widow. Psalm 146:9

"Become like Little Children"

Share these words with your grandparents:

I tell you the truth, unless you change and become like little children, you will never enter the kingdom of heaven. Matthew 18:3

Then challenge them to "become like little children" by doing something spontaneous with you.

A "Good Husband," a "Good Wife"

The following autograph was found in a 100-year-old autograph book:

> May you always be happy
> Each day of your life,
> Get a good husband,
> And make a good wife.

Ask your grandparents to share with you what they think makes "a good husband" and "a good wife."

Have the Tables Turned?

Years ago grandparents spoiled their grandchildren while parents disciplined their children. According to some, it is now reversed. Today, grandparents are forced to discipline grandchildren while parents spoil them. Ask your grandparents what they think.

"Wherever You Go …"

Remind your grandparents, "Wherever you go, you take yourself with you." Sometimes when one loses a spouse, one wants to forget. You make a move or marry another person too quickly, forgetting that you can't runaway from your sorrow, your loneliness.

269 "Do What You Can ..."

Theodore Roosevelt once said, "Do what you can, with what you have, where you are." Ask your grandparents to tell you what they think you can do, with "what you have, where you are."

270 A Challenge to Stop "Should-ing"

Challenge your grandparents to stop "should-ing." We have a peculiar habit of always "should-ing" ourselves: "We should have done this," "We should have done that," or "We should be in there washing the dishes."

271 A Thought about Life

Remind your grandparents of what Adlai Stevenson once said, "It is not the years of your life but the life in your years that counts."

272 Overlooking

Someone once said, "The art of being wise is the art of knowing what to overlook." Ask your grandparents what kinds of things they think you should overlook.

A Reminder about Laughter

Make a sign for your grandparents with the following saying on it: "A day is lost if one has not laughed."

A Reminder That God Keeps His Promises

Remind your grandparents that God keeps His every promise:

Know therefore that the LORD your God is God; He is the faithful God, keeping His covenant of love to a thousand generations of those who love Him and keep His commands. Deuteronomy 7:9

When a Friends Dies

When your grandparents lose a friend, share with them the comforting words of John 14:1–6:

"Do not let your hearts be troubled. Trust in God; trust also in Me. In My Father's house are many rooms; if it were not so, I would have told you. I am going there to prepare a place for you. And if I go and prepare a place for you, I will come back and take you to be with Me that you also may be where I am. You know the way to the place where I am going." Thomas said to Him, "Lord, we don't

know where You are going, so how can we know the way?" Jesus answered, "I am the way and the truth and the life. No one comes to the Father except through Me."

Your Grandparents' Love

Thank your grandparents for all the love they give you. Tell them their love is described in these words:

Love is patient, love is kind. It does not envy, it does not boast, it is not proud. It is not rude, it is not self-seeking, it is not easily angered, it keeps no record of wrongs. Love does not delight in evil but rejoices with the truth. It always protects, always trusts, always hopes, always perseveres. Love never fails. 1 Corinthians 13:4–8b

Don't Give Up!

Anyone can get discouraged at times, including your grandparents. Remind them of God's promise:

Let us not become weary in doing good, for at the proper time we will reap a harvest if we do not give up. Galatians 6:9

A Reminder of What Awaits the Faithful

Remind your grandparents of what awaits the faithful:

Be faithful, even to the point of death, and I will give you the crown of life. Revelation 2:10c

A Testimony of Faith

Remind your grandparents why you love the Word of God by sharing with them the words of Romans 1:16:

I am not ashamed of the gospel, because it is the power of God for the salvation of everyone who believes.

When Excited about a Special Blessing

As you share with your grandparents about some special blessing you have received, share the words of the psalmist with them:

Praise the LORD, for the LORD is good. Psalm 135:3a

A Happy Family

Remind your grandparents of this truth: "A happy family is but an earlier heaven."

A Tape Measure around the Heart

Remind your grandparents that someone once said, "When God measures man, He puts the tape around his heart, not his head." Tell them, however, as far as you're concerned, no tape measure is big enough to measure around their hearts.

The Importance of Reading

Ask your grandparents which books they've read that they think you absolutely must read.

Bible Trivia

Read Ezra 7:21–22 with your grandparents, and see who can guess which letter of the alphabet is missing.

The Longest and the Shortest

Read with your grandparents the longest verse and the shortest chapter in the Bible (the longest verse: Esther 8:9; the shortest chapter: Psalm 117).

Ask Them to Explain

Ask your grandparents to explain the statement, "I have read many books, but the Bible reads me."

A Special Blessing

Buy a blank card, then write the following blessing for your grandparents:

The Lord bless you, and keep you;
The Lord make His face to shine on you,
and be gracious to you;
the Lord lift up His countenance on you,
and give you peace. Numbers 6:24–26 (NASB)

When Life Seems All Tangled Up

When everything seems to be going wrong for a grandparent, share with him or her something you've learned: "When life becomes all snarled up, offer it to the Lord and let Him untie the knots."

How to Trap an Atheist

Tell your grandparents you heard a truth that you'd like to share with them: "How to trap an atheist: Serve him a fine meal, then ask him if he believes there is a cook." Then ask them if they have any secrets to witnessing to an atheist.

Ask Your Grandpa

Ask your grandpa if he has any thoughts on Proverbs 21:19:

Better to live in a desert than with a quarrelsome and ill-tempered wife.

Remind him that the same truth might hold for someone who has to live with a quarrelsome and ill-tempered husband.

Do They Agree?

Remind your grandparents that someone once said, "old age was 15 years older than (he was)." Ask them what they think "old age" is.

What Is a Home?

If you have spent a great deal of time with your grandparents, or if your grandparents' home was your home (for whatever reason), give them a special sign that reads: "This is a home that our feet may leave, but not our hearts."

The Ability to See Beauty

If it seems as if your grandparents are always seeing the positive and good, thank them, then remind them of the saying of Franz Kafka, "Youth is happy because it has the ability to see beauty. Anyone who keeps the ability to see beauty never grows old."

When Feeling Bad about a Mistake

Remind your grandma, when she is worrying about something she's done wrong, that "God has a big eraser." You might want to remind her by sending her an actual eraser with this message printed on the top of it.

Do They Remember?

Ask your grandparents if they have heard Franklin D. Roosevelt's statement, "The only thing we have to fear is fear itself." Ask them to explain it to you.

When They Say It's Miserable Growing Old

When they tell you it's miserable to grow old, remind your grandparents that "old age isn't so bad when you consider the alternative." (Maurice Chevalier)

Shutting the Devil Out

Remind your grandparents of what Martin Luther said: "The devil does not stay where music is." Then invite them to spend some time with you, listening to some great music!

Love Them
by Sharing Time

Too often, one hears stories of people who wished they had spent more time with their loved ones before they died. My son always saw the time he spent with Grandpa Sonnenberg as "grand." A few hours after we learned my father had died, my wife found Jacob, our son, "Grandpa's fishing buddy," sitting on the floor in his bedroom with his fishing tackle box open. He was holding in his hand the fishing plug his grandpa had sent him the previous Christmas. It was obvious he had been crying. Robin sat beside him on the floor and hugged him.

"You know, Mom, Grandpa gave me his very favorite fishing plug. He told me ... he told me in the garage last summer, when just him and me sat in the garage ... he told me about all the fish this plug caught ... he told me ..." Tears began to well up in Jacob's eyes.

Nothing more needed to be said. For Jacob, it was a time to remember. A time to remember precious time spent with his grandpa, time that now meant the world to him. Precious time that was meaningful not only to Jacob, but had been to Grandpa Sonnenberg as well. It was that time spent in the garage one summer afternoon with his grandson from California that moved him to take a special fishing plug out of his tackle box, carefully wrap it, and send it as a Christmas gift. For Jacob, the fishing plug became a visual reminder of

114

the very last visit he had with his grandpa. It was a time when he and Grandpa were one in spirit—fishermen with dreams of catching even "bigger ones" than they had caught before. It is a memory of a moment that will last a lifetime. A "grand" time between a "grandchild" and his "grandpa." A memory, a hug from the past.

An Invitation to Be Silly

As we grow older, we sometimes lose the sense of silliness. It's almost as if we think it's inappropriate to be silly as we mature. Invite your grandparents to do something silly and funny, like run together in the rain or have a water balloon fight.

Read a Book to Them

Why not ask your grandparents if you can tuck them into bed and read them your favorite bedtime story? Choose one of your favorite books to read or a portion of the Bible.

Guess Who's Coming to Dinner

Ask your grandparents to write down their favorite meal, then prepare the meal for them. Guaranteed, they'll appreciate all your efforts and hard work.

301 Take Me to the Movies

Invite your grandparents to the movies. Pick up videos of old movies that were popular when they were younger. Buy some popcorn and sodas. Invite them over to your place or go to their place (if they have a VCR) and watch the movies. Be sure to dim the lights and serve treats.

302 Join in Working a Jigsaw Puzzle

Buy a large jigsaw puzzle, and spend time with your grandparents putting the puzzle together. As you join together in joining the puzzle, talk and laugh with one another.

303 Sunrise, Sunset

Invite your grandparents to watch a sunrise or a sunset (or both) with you.

304 "Couch Potato"

A "couch potato" is someone who sits on the couch and does nothing but watch TV. Challenge your grandparents to join you in doing something more productive and healthy than being couch potatoes. Invite them to visit the library with you and to research some interesting subject.

Treating Them like Adults

If your grandparents are not as alert as they used to be because of memory or hearing loss, pledge not to talk down to them as if they were children. Talk to and treat them like adults.

What Do You Think, Grandpa?

Other than the Bible, do books written years ago have something relevant for us today? The following quote came from a book in one grandpa's library. Ask your grandparents to comment on it.

> I have a profound admiration for the Skunk. Indeed, I once maintained that this animal was the proper emblem of America. It is, first of all, peculiar to this continent. It has stars on its head and stripes on its body. It is an ideal citizen; minds its own business, harms no one, and is habitually inoffensive, as long as it is left alone; but it will face anyone or any number of adversaries when aroused. It has a wonderful natural ability to take the offensive; and no man ever yet came to grips with a Skunk without being sadly sorry for it afterward.

Nevertheless, in spite of all this, and the fact that several other countries have prior claims on the Eagle, I could not secure, for my view, sufficient popular support to change the national emblem.[3]

Be a Stargazer

Sit outside with your grandparents on a warm summer night and watch for shooting stars.

Walk, Walk, Walk

Invite your grandparents to take a walk with you. If it's summer, walk around the block. If it's winter, take them to the mall to walk. Whenever or wherever the walk is taking place, make sure you are considerate of them. They may be slower than you.

Do Something Different

The next time you spend a weekend with your grandparents, encourage them to do something wacky and different, such as eating ice cream for breakfast or playing in the rain and splashing each other in the mud puddles.

Rest and Be Thankful

Go to an area park or out on the front porch. Sit down with your grandparents and do exactly what an inscription on a stone seat in the Scottish Highlands says:

"Rest and be thankful."

A Day Together

If your grandparents live far away, do something together with them on the same day, such as arranging to go to the same movie or a similar restaurant at the same time. Then talk to each other the next day via the telephone, fax, or e-mail to compare notes. What did you like about the movie? dislike?

Arranging in Advance

Someone has said, "You must arrange in advance for pleasant memories." Help your grandparents arrange for some pleasant memories by challenging them to memorize with you some key Bible verses about life and death.

What then shall we say in response to this? If God is for us, who can be against us? He who did not spare His own Son, but gave Him up for us all—how will He not also, along with Him, graciously give us all things? Who will bring any charge against those whom God has chosen? It is God who justifies. Who is he that condemns? Christ Jesus, who died—more than that, who was raised to life—is at the right hand of God and is also interceding for us. Who shall separate us from the love of Christ? Shall trouble or hardship or perse-cution or famine or nakedness or danger or sword? ... No, in all these things we are more than conquerors through Him who loved us. For I am convinced that neither death nor life, neither angels nor demons, neither the present nor the future, nor any powers, neither height nor depth, nor anything else in all creation, will be able to separate us from the love of God that is in Christ Jesus our Lord. (Romans 8:31–39)

Have a contest. See who can memorize the most vers-es or the fastest. Celebrate no matter how many verses you've memorized; you've made some arrangements for some pleasant memories, maybe even when you close your eyelids in death and remember that "nothing ... even death" can separate you from Christ.

Blow Bubbles

Buy two bottles of bubbles and sit on the front porch of your grandparents' home and blow bubbles. Laugh and chase the bubbles.

Match the Socks

Invite your grandparents to play a game with you called "Match the Socks." Get all the socks you can find, put them in a pile, and see which player is able to match up the most pairs in a given amount of time.

Sign "I Love You"

Sometimes older people are unable to say anything because of a stroke or heart attack. Practice saying "I love you" in sign language so if that time ever comes, you can express your love to your grandparents. You will, of course, want to learn the sign language together and say it often to one another before such a time might occur.

 I  L O V E  Y O U

Quality Time

One of the primary love languages Gary Chapman speaks of in his book, *The Five Love Languages*, is "quality time." Resolve to speak this love language to your grandparents (meet them for breakfast at a local restaurant, take time to help your grandpa mow his backyard).

Physical Touch

Another of the love languages Gary Chapman speaks of in his book, *The Five Love Languages*, is "physical touch." Resolve to speak this love language to your grandparents (hug your grandpa when he comes to your soccer game, hold your grandma's hands as you pray together).

Build a Sand Castle

Pack a lunch, put on your sun attire, and bring some comfortable beach chairs and a nice umbrella. Then invite your grandpa to build a sand castle with you.

Before Television

If your grandparents are old enough to have lived before television, ask them to tell you about some of the more memorable things they did before TV's heyday. Then ask them to spend a night doing those things with you.

"I Love You" in French

The French are considered romantic people. Practice saying "I love you" in French, then say it often to your grandparents: *je t'aime*, which sounds like "zhe tem."

Play and Talk

The next time you visit your grandparents' home overnight, ask them if you can play a board game with them instead of watching television.

T-I-M-E

T-I-M-E spells love. Spend time listening to your grandparents. Remember, when you give them, or anyone, time, you give them life. Time is life!

Pass on a Tradition

Show your grandparents that you appreciate their gifts and talents by asking them to teach you what they know. For example, if your grandma crochets, ask her to teach you how to do it. If your grandpa is a craftsman, ask if you can spend some time building something.

"Backwards Day"

Ask your grandparents if they'd like to do something different. Tell them the next time you spend a day with them, you'd like to break the routine of things! Eat lunch for breakfast. Start with dessert before the main course. Drink your soup. Be creative. Ask them to help you think of things you could do "backwards." The purpose? Just to have some fun, to be silly, to get out of the normal routine of things.

A Random Act of Kindness

A bumper sticker reads, "Practice random acts of kindness and senseless acts of beauty." Take time this week to practice a random act of kindness toward your grandparents. Surprise your grandpa by washing his car. Call your grandma and tell her why you love her.

Time to Grieve

If your grandparent loses a spouse, expect and affirm his or her grief. Remember, very few of us have experienced what they have! Often our grandparents have been married for years—sometimes 50 years or more. They may not remember life apart from each other. Though we may not know what they're going through, remind them Who does:

> *For we do not have a high priest who is unable to sympathize with our weaknesses, but we have one who has been tempted in every way, just as we are—yet was without sin. Let us then approach the throne of grace with confidence, so that we may receive mercy and find grace to help us in our time of need.* (Hebrews 4:15–16)

124

Give them a copy of *Good Grief* by Granger Westberg (Philadelphia, PA: Fortress Press, 1986). The book is short and deals with the different stages of grief: shock, expression of emotion, loneliness, physical symptoms of distress, panic, guilt, anger, resentment, resistance to returning, hope. Watch for excessive behavior patterns that may be harmful, such as alcohol abuse or severe depression.

327 Catalogue Shopping

Sit with your grandma and leaf through a catalogue. Wish together what you'd like from each page. Make sure you let your grandma wish with you.

328 A Night Alone

Make a bonfire by a lake or ocean and toast marshmallows, just you and your grandpa and grandma.

329 The Present of Presence

Anyone can buy a present for your grandparents. The best present you can give your grandparents, one only you can give, is your "presence." Make some arrangements to give this present to them soon.

Look beyond the Behavior

Parents are reminded by the experts to look beyond the behavior of their child by asking such questions as, "Why is he behaving in such a way?" or "What's made her so cranky?" The next time your grandpa behaves in a way that upsets you, look beyond the behavior. Give him the benefit of the doubt. Take some time to step back and reflect on why he might be acting a certain way, then "put the best construction" on his behavior.

Cuddle and Talk

The next time it's cold and you're with your grandparents, cuddle together under a warm blanket on the couch and talk.

Count the People Smiling

Sit on a bench with your grandparents and count the number of people who are smiling as they pass by. Talk to your grandparents about smiling and what they've learned about smiling over the years.

Choose Conversation over Television

The next time you're with your grandparents, choose conversation over television.

Auto Mechanics

Ask your grandpa to tell you what he knows about the basic maintenance of an automobile, such as changing the oil, checking the transmission fluid, checking the tire pressure, etc.

Who'll Cry First?

Challenge your grandma to a contest. Peel an onion together and see who cries first! After the onion is peeled, make onion soup, an onion sandwich, or onion rings.

Retreat Together

Sneak away from home some day with your grandpa and find a tree to sit under. Enjoy the sounds and smells around you, and perhaps read a book together.

337

Savor the Moment and the Taste

Buy a special candy bar, then invite your grandma to eat it with you. Pledge to savor every bite of it. To do this, tell her that together you will take exactly 29 bites as you eat it.

338

Stop to Enjoy

Take a walk and stop often to smell the roses, the lemons on the tree, the freshly mown hay, etc.

339

Don't Let Go

The next time you and your grandpa hug, let him be the first to let go.

340

Don't Whine

The next time you're with your grandparents, don't whine or complain about anything.

341

"How Can I Help?"

The next time your grandma seems to be feeling down, ask, "How can I help?"

A Special Baseball Game

Take your grandpa to see his favorite baseball, basketball, or football team play.

Whistle a Happy Tune

Ask your grandpa to whistle the tune to a television program and he will more than likely remember, "The Andy Griffith Show." Whistle it together. Whistle it at your next family gathering.

Break the Routine

Talk to your grandparents about "routine" and ask them what things they do that they know are routine. Then invite them to do something out of the routine, such as early breakfast at a restaurant instead of the usual 7:30 A.M. breakfast at home.

Do Nothing

Invite your grandparents to spend 30 minutes with you "doing nothing."

Swing Together

Invite your grandma to a nearby park to swing with you. Be sure she gets her chance to swing. As you swing, sing "Amazing Grace" together.

Smell the Flowers

Go to the country with your grandparents. Find a field and walk in it. When you find a patch of wild flowers, smell them, then sit down next to them, or in them, and talk to one another.

Two Generations—One Book

Choose a book you could read together with your grandpa. Purchase two copies, one for you and another for him. Over the next several weeks, read the book separately. Then after you're finished, discuss it.

Play with Modeling Clay

Purchase some modeling clay and invite your grandparents to create monsters with you.

An Act of Childhood

Invite your grandparents to the local park and ride the merry-go-round together.

An Invitation to Dream

Invite your grandparents to sit by the fireplace and dream with you. Talk about what each of you is looking forward to. What do you want out of life? Share your personal dreams with one another!

Take a Nap Together

Someone once said, "No day is so bad it can't be fixed by a nap." The next time you're with your grandparents and they seem to be having a hard day, remind them of this saying, and then take a nap together.

Sing Aloud

The next time you're alone in the car with your grandparents, ask them to join you in singing with the radio or a cassette you've brought along. Sing with abandon! Sing not to receive musical acclaim, but simply for enjoyment and fellowship.

Spending the Afternoon

Someone once said, "You should spend the afternoon because you can't take it with you." Invite your grandparents to do that very thing with you soon. Do something that might seem like a "perfect waste of time."

Bike Ride in the Rain

Go for a bike ride in the rain.

Turn Off the Radio

The next time you're in the car with your grandparents, ask if you can turn off the radio so you can talk. Then talk … about each other's dreams, each other's hopes, each other's concerns.

A Special Bible Verse

Choose a special Bible verse to use as a family motto, then memorize it together.

An Afternoon Tea

Take your grandma out for afternoon tea at a fancy restaurant—just the two of you. Enjoy the little sandwiches, the soft music, and each other's company.

A Special Quality

The next time you're with your grandpa, tell him the one special quality you like best about him (i.e., that he's honest, kind, etc.).

Read the Funny Papers

Read the comics with your grandparents.

Unplug the Clock

The next time you're with your grandparents, see if they'll let you unplug the clock for a whole day. Then agree not to worry about time.

Throw Snowballs

On a cold wintry day, invite your grandpa to bundle up and go outside with you to throw snowballs at each other.

Play the Kazoo

Purchase some inexpensive kazoos and ask your grand-parents to play a tune with you. Record your music, and listen to it together. Laugh and enjoy the silliness of the whole thing.

Listen to a Seashell

Go to the ocean together and look for seashells. Put them to your ears and listen for the different sounds.

Memorize a Poem

Choose a poem to memorize together, then share it at your next family gathering.

A Special Backrub

Give your grandma a special backrub. Use your finger to draw out the letters of I love you on her back.

Say It in German

Surprise your grandparents with "I love you" in German. It is *Ich liebe dich,* which sounds like "Ick leebe dick."

Volunteer Together

One survey showed that one out of every five Americans did some volunteer work for a church or other charitable agency. Ask your grandparents if they'd like to do volunteer work with you.

Bird-watching

Purchase a book from your local Audubon Society or bookstore on birds. Then invite your grandparents to go bird-watching with you.

Speak Their Language

If your grandparents speak a language other than English, ask them to teach you some phrases. Ask especially to learn "I love you," and "I'm so happy to see you."

Walk and Hold Hands

Invite your grandparents to go to the local mall and browse. As you do, hold hands with them.

Love Them by Sharing Something Handmade

A busy father decided to record bedtime stories for his daughter so when she wanted to hear the stories, she could listen to them over and over again. One night he found her crying. He asked why. She said, "Daddy, I don't like these stories anymore. I want stories with skin on them." She needed something more important than the bedtime stories. She needed her daddy next to her telling the stories.

In a sense, handmade crafts are like that. They are gifts with "skin on them." They give a special message of love! For many people, it is easy to buy something to give someone, but to make a gift adds a special touch.

Some ideas for handmade gifts are suggested below; most of them can be done by younger children. They provide special ways to express love to grandparents.

 372

"Jesus Loves"

Materials:
Picture frame
Aluminum foil

Buy an inexpensive picture frame. Cut out letters or draw on paper the words, "Jesus Loves." Put the aluminum foil inside the picture frame and paste the letters "Jesus Loves" along the top edge of the aluminum foil. Send the picture to your grandparents. Ask them to look into the frame, and, as they see their faces on the shiny aluminum foil, be reminded that Jesus loves them.

Jesus Loves Our Family

Materials:
Jar
Marbles
A branch
White paper
Scissors
Markers or crayons
Yarn
Glue
Hole punch
Tape
Construction paper

Everyone needs to be reminded time and time again that Jesus loves them—young and old. Make a special gift for your grandparents to remind them that Jesus loves them and every member of the family.

Cut a heart from construction paper. Write "Jesus

Loves Our Family" on the heart. Paste it on the jar. Fill the jar with marbles (or pebbles). Place the branch in the jar. (The marbles should hold it tight.) Cut out hearts from the white paper. Draw faces of each member of your family on the individual hearts. Use yarn to add hair. Punch a hole at the top of each heart. Loop yarn through the hole and hang it on the branch. By the time you're through, you should have one heart for every member of the family.

 374

God—Keeper of All Promises

Materials:

A sheet of blue construction paper

Different colored yarn

Glue

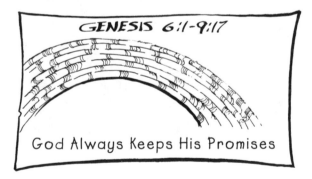

GENESIS 6:1-9:17

God Always Keeps His Promises

Scripture includes many promises from God. Remind your grandparents of one such promise by making a rainbow.

Cut different lengths of yarn, depending on where you want each piece to fit into the rainbow. The colors that appear in a rainbow are red, orange, yellow, green, blue, indigo, and violet. (However, you don't need all these colors to make the rainbow.)

Glue the different pieces of yarn onto the blue construction paper, making a rainbow.

Give it to your grandparents, reminding them that God promised Noah He would never send a terrible flood again on the earth. He said a rainbow would remind all the people of the world of His promise (Genesis 6:1–9:17).

Tell them that, just as God kept that promise, so we can be assured He'll keep every promise He has ever made, including the one about eternal life for all believers in Christ Jesus.

A Rubber Stamp Bookmark

Materials:

Card stock (any color)

Rubber stamp (your choice)

Pinking shears

Clear adhesive (or have the bookmark laminated at the local quick copy store)

1 12" length of braid, glossy cord, or rope for tassel

Hole punch

Cut a bookmark out of card stock using the following pattern or your own. Trim the top and bottom of the bookmark with pinking shears.

Decorate with the rubber stamp or draw a picture on it.

Print a Bible verse and special message on the bookmark. Laminate it at your local quick copy store or seal it with clear adhesive. Trim the sides to finish.

Punch a hole in the top and thread braid or rope tassel through the hole and tie. Fringe or fray ends and knot.

376

Scripture Paperweight

Materials:

Flat smooth rock (beach or river stones are especially good)

Fine-tip paintbrush

2 or 3 colors of craft paint

Fine-tip permanent marking pen

Spray-on varnish (optional)

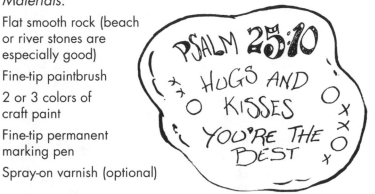

Wash the rock thoroughly and dry it.

Choose a special Scripture verse and paint it on the rock. Add your own artwork to personalize. (Make sure you wash and dry your brush between color changes.)

Spray with varnish. Spray on several coats, allowing each coat to dry thoroughly before you spray on the next.

377

Family Tree—"Thanks for Giving Us Roots"

Materials:

Small clay pot

Oasis or green Styrofoam

Spanish moss or peat moss

Green construction paper

Scissors

(Optional) Instead of cutting leaves from green construction paper, purchase a small bag of wooden tear drops from any craft store

Green paint for leaves (if using wooden tear drops)

Fine-tip permanent marker

Small tree branch with plenty of little limbs (It's fun to find this limb together as you and your grandparents take a walk.)

Glue or glue gun

Glue the Styrofoam or oasis in the clay pot. Spread glue on the bottom portion of the tree branch and push it into the Styrofoam. Glue the moss around the base of the tree. Let dry until firm.

As the glue dries, paint the wooden leaves with green paint or cut leaves from the green construction paper.

After the paint has dried or the leaves have been cut out, write each family member's name on a separate leaf. Glue these leaves to the tree branches. (You can place married family members together by gluing two teardrops together in the shape of a heart.)

Finally, print the following saying around the rim of the clay pot:

"Thanks for Giving Us Roots!"

144

378 Sunshine Flowerpot

Materials:

Spanish moss

3" clay flowerpot

White craft paint (water-base)

Large silk sunflower with sturdy stem

Styrofoam

Sponge

Glue gun or glue

Permanent black marker

Using a small dry sponge, take small amounts of white craft paint and sponge the exterior of the clay pot. Leave portions of clay color showing through the white paint to make a stippled effect.

After the pot has dried, print the following around the pot's rim:

"You Are My Sunshine"

Glue Styrofoam and the silk sunflower into the clay pot. Finish by gluing the moss on top of the pot.

379

Angelic Recyclable

DEAR GRANDMA AND GRANDPA, WHEN THIS YOU SEE PLEASE THINK OF ME. I LOVE YOU. ...ELLEN

Materials:

Soda can

Glue gun

Curly doll hair (any color, available at a craft store)

White spray paint

Transparent glitter

Gold tinsel chenille wire

12" of 2"-wide elegant wire ribbon (white or gold moiré or satin)

Fine-tip permanent marker

Wrapping paper

Remove flip top from the soda can and discard. Spray paint the soda can, making sure to completely cover the can. Before it dries, shake the glitter over the entire can, then let it dry.

Gently bend the can in half until the mouth (top) of the can is looking at you. If necessary, touch up with additional spray paint and glitter where needed.

Take a fine-tip marker and draw eyelids and lashes on the face. Use a little lipstick to make rosy cheeks. The pour spout of the can is the mouth.

Make a halo from the chenille wire. Glue it to the top rim of the can.

Take a small clump of curly hair and glue it on top of the can around the base of the halo.

Shape wire ribbon into a pretty bow. The bow should project enough from the sides of the can to look like angel wings. Glue the bow to the back center of the can.

Cut a tag from the wrapping paper and print the following message:

> Dear Grandma and Grandpa,
> When this you see,
> Please think of me.
> I love you.
> *Your Name*

A Shining Star Ornament

Materials:

Craft foam or construction board (light color)

Hole punch

Fine-tip permanent marker

Glue (clear drying)

Paintbrush

Transparent glitter

Ribbon (any color)

Trace the pattern of a star onto the craft foam or construction board. Cut it out.

Punch a hole in the top of one point. Write on it: "Grandpa, you are a shining star!" with the permanent pen.

Use a fine-tip pen to draw a stitching border around the star.

Paint a thin coat of glue over the star and sprinkle lightly with transparent glitter.

Finish by tying a ribbon through the hole so it can be an ornament on a Christmas tree, a window, or a doorknob, etc.

Somebunny Special

Materials:

Craft foam or felt (white for body; pink for inside ears, cheeks, and toes)

Construction paper or felt (pink for grandma, blue for grandpa)

Ribbon (pink for grandma, blue for grandpa)

Glue

Cotton balls

Fine-tip permanent marker

Trace the whole body pattern (pattern on page 150) onto the white craft foam or felt. Then trace the small pieces (ears, cheeks, toes onto the pink craft foam or felt). Then trace the egg onto the blue or pink construction paper or felt. Cut out all the patterns. Then cut an opening on the feet and hands where the egg is to be inserted (note the dotted lines).

Glue all the pieces together. Then tie a small bow using pink or blue ribbon and glue it on the neckline. Write with a fine-tip marker the following message on the egg:

"Grandma, you are somebunny special."

Finish by using the fine-tip marker to make eyes, mouth, and wrinkles around the toes.

Praise Box

Materials:

A box of any shape or size

Magazines (that you can cut up)

Scissors

Glue

Small slips of paper, big enough for written messages of love

Pen

A piece of ribbon long enough to wrap around the box and make into a pretty bow

Flip through the magazines and find pictures that remind you of your grandparents. Cut them out and glue them onto the box.

Take the small slips of paper and write notes or messages praising your grandpa and grandma. For example: "Grandma, you bake the best chocolate-chip cookies in the world!" or "Grandpa, I love the way you always take time to listen to me!"

Tie the box up with a pretty ribbon and bow and present it to your grandparents with love. Tell them that they can read the notes of love whenever they need a lift.

383 Measuring Magnet

Materials:

Plain wooden ruler (cut in half) or any color craft foam

Black permanent marker

Long magnet strip

Cut a wooden ruler in half or trace a ruler onto a piece of craft foam and cut it out (make sure to add the measurements of a ruler).

Write with a permanent marker:

"Grandpa, I hope I'll measure up to you."

Glue the magnet strip onto the back.

384 Fingerprint Refrigerator Magnet

Materials:

Craft foam or poster board (red, white, brown)

Inkpad

Glue

Magnet
strip

Fine-tip
perma-
nent
marker

Using either craft foam or poster board, cut a house out of the white, a roof from the brown, and a heart from the red. Glue the roof and the heart onto the house.

Fingerprint each family member and press onto the white house.

Use a fine-tip marking pen to make a happy face out of each fingerprint, then write the person's name next to his or her face.

Glue the magnet onto the back of the house.

385 A "Bearing My Love" Magnet

Materials:

Brown construction paper

Brown puffy paint

Black marker

White card stock

Trace the bear pattern onto brown construction paper and cut out.

Outline the bear with brown puffy paint. Cut out the bear's sign from white card stock, then write on the sign the following words:

"Bearing my love! *Your Name*"

386

Family Hands Wreath

Materials:

Green construction paper or craft foam

Different colors of construction paper or craft foam

Glue

Fine-tip permanent marker

Dinner plate

Trace a circle on the green craft foam or construction paper using the dinner plate (this will be the wreath). Then ask each member of the family to trace his or her hand onto a different color of construction paper or craft foam (make several prints of each person). You might even want the paw prints of your animals. Ask each member of the family to sign his or her name on the handprints.

Cut out the handprints, place them around the wreath, and glue them down.

Make a banner from red foam or construction paper and personalize. Glue the banner to the wreath. Then send it with love to your grandparents.

387 Bound-by-Love Books

Materials:

3 old books (bindings must be 1″ wide or wider)

1 to 1 ½ yards of 2″– to 3″– wide wire ribbon (solid or print)

Silk flowers or dried greenery

Glue gun

Black marking pen

White or cream colored card stock

Wrap ribbon around the books both horizontally and vertically, like wrapping a gift. Tie a pretty bow on top and shape.

Cut a tag from the card stock and print on it:

"Our family is bound by love."

Then glue the flowers and tag to the top of the books.

A "Migh-tea" Special Refrigerator Magnet

Materials:

Craft foam

Fine-tip black marker

Black fine-tip puffy paint

Tea bag

Magnet strip

Trace the following teapot pattern onto craft foam and cut it out.

Then print "Grandma, you are 'migh-tea' special!" on the teapot.

Outline the black areas with puffy paint.

Glue the magnet strip onto the back.

Place a tea bag and the "Migh-tea" magnet into an envelope and send it to your grandma!

389 Love Note Stocking

Materials:

Small Christmas stocking (one that can be hung on the tree)

Small sheet of paper

Pen

Write a special love note to your grandparents and tuck it inside the stocking. Be sure to date the note.

Put the stocking into a little envelope and mail it with love to your grandparents.

They might want to share the tradition with you by sending you a love note packaged in a small stocking. These little stocking can be cherished heirlooms for years to come.

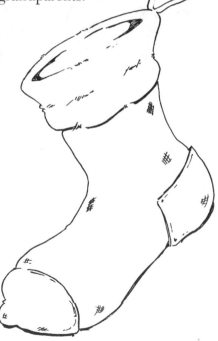

390

Joy Wall Hanging

Materials:

Craft foam or construction paper

Small photo of yourself

Puffy paint

Permanent marker

Embroidery floss, yarn, or string

Trace the pattern onto craft foam or construction paper and cut it out. Cut out the center "O" as an opening for your picture. Glue the picture into the opening. Decorate the letters with puffy paint and allow them to dry. Write the following words on the heart using the permanent marker:

"Grandma, you fill my heart with joy."

Tie the heart onto the bottom of the "O" using the embroidery floss, yarn, or string.

391 Child's Handprint or Footprint Plaque

Materials:

A large lump of make-and-bake clay (any color)

Ribbon

Toothpick

Take a piece of clay large enough to accommodate your child's footprint or handprint. Flatten the dough into the desired shape. Press your child's hand or foot into the clay until a good imprint is visible.

Poke two large holes at the top of the plaque. Make sure they are large enough to accommodate the ribbon.

Use the toothpick to etch your child's name and the date into the plaque. Bake at 250° for approximately 15 minutes. After the plaque has cooled, string the ribbon through the holes and tie tightly at the top.

 ## 392 "Hands Down" T-Shirt or Sweatshirt

Materials:

T-shirt or sweatshirt

Fabric craft paints (any color)

Pie tins for each color of paint

Black permanent fabric marker (calligraphy tip is great)

Paper towels

Pre-wash the T-shirt or sweatshirt. Put the paints into separate pie tins. Place your child's hand into the paint. Blot

off excess paint using the paper towels. Press your child's hand onto the T-shirt. Repeat the process until you have several handprints on the shirt. Let dry.

Finally, using the fabric marker, print "Grandpa, hands down you're the greatest!"

More Precious than Real Money

Materials:
Cardboard
Scissors
Pen

Cut some large coins out of cardboard. Then print on them things such as:

Good for one big kiss!

Good for one long hug!

Good for one good vacuum cleaning of the living room.

Good for a long talk!

394 "This Is How Big I Am!"

Materials:
Butcher Paper
Crayons
Colored mark-
ers

Get a large sheet of paper, large enough to trace your entire body on. Lie down on the paper, and with a large crayon or marker, have someone trace all the way around you. Cut out the life-sized body double. With crayons or colored markers, decorate it with clothes, etc. Send it to your grandparents, telling them since you can't be there in person all the time, you can at least be there life-sized in paper!

You might tell your grandparents that you'd sure like it if they sent you the same "pictures" for your wall!

An Edible Necklace for Grandma

Materials:

Alphabet cereal

Clean thread or plain dental floss

Miniature marshmallows

Needle

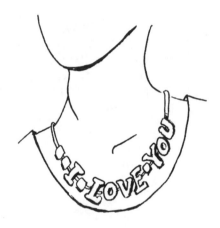

Take a large needle and clean thread and string a message onto the string using the alphabet letters. How about, "I love you" or "You're Number One"? Place one or two miniature marshmallows between each letter to help space out the letters (this makes it easier to read). Tell your grandma that if she gets hungry someday, she should feel free to eat the necklace (but not the string)!

Love Them by Sharing Thoughts

We sometimes forget that everyone needs to know they are loved—grandparents too! They need to be hugged and kissed; they need to hear "I love you" and "You never cease to amaze me with your wisdom." Though there are countless books on loving your wife, husband, grandchildren, there are few books about loving your grandparents. But grandparents are people too!

Experts tell us everyone—young and old—needs the following things for their well-being, their sense of self-worth: *competence*, a feeling that one is capable, knowing that one can do something well; *worth*, a feeling that one is acceptable, knowing that what one feels and thinks is important; and *belonging*, a feeling of community, knowing one is part of something bigger than himself or herself. The purpose of this section is to help you love your grandparents by giving them a sense of competence, worth, and belonging. For example, one of the suggested ways of loving your grandparents is to ask them what they think about God, Jesus, sin, forgiveness, and eternal life. In listening to them, you honor them. You give them a sense of worth. You are saying, "What you say is important. What you think is valuable."

396 "The Best Is Yet to Come"

Few things are more valuable to receive from one's grandparents than encouragement, encouragement for the present, as well as the future.

One wise grandmother told her grandchildren that she wanted to be buried with two things in her hands. In one, she wanted her worn-out Bible; in the other, she wanted a fork—one of the fine, sterling silver forks straight out of the set her mother had handed down to her.

The daughter asked why she wanted to be buried with a fork in her hand.

"When I was growing up, at very special meals, the hostess would come behind you and, after picking up your empty plate would say, 'You may keep your fork.' We knew what that meant. It meant dessert was on its way. Not just ordinary dessert, but more than likely homemade pie or cake. The best was yet to come!"

One of the grandchildren said, "I still don't get it, Grandma. Why the fork in your hand when you're dead and about to be buried?"

"You must explain why to those who pass by the casket, my dear," she answered, "I want you and the rest of the grandchildren to stand next to the casket, and try not to shed a tear. When those who pass by ask about the fork, I want you to say, 'Because for Grandma, the best has come!' "

Grandchildren are not the only people who need to hear, "The best is yet to come." Sometimes grandparents also need to be reminded. Tell your grandparents the story and share with them the same truth, that for Christians, death means "the best has come."

"Olive You"

Tell the following "knock, knock" joke to your grand-parents.

> *Knock, knock.*
> Who's there?
> *Olive*
> Olive who?
> *Olive you!*

Your Idea of Life

Get a business card from either your dad or mom (or from someone else who has one). Give it to your grandpa, telling him: "Someone once said, 'If you can't write an idea on the back of a business card, you don't have a good idea.' I'm sending you this business card to prove that you've got lots of good ideas. I'd like you to write one of these ideas on the back of this business card."

Can You Describe Such a Time?

Tell your grandparents you heard once that "what a caterpillar sees as a tragedy, the butterfly sees as a master-piece." Ask if they can remember a time when something seemed like a real tragedy, but turned out to be a masterpiece.

Growth 400

Years ago, before the day and age of dentists and "false teeth," the Eskimos would be forced to abandon the aged who had lost their teeth and were unable to eat the staple of that day—the tough meat of wild animals.

One day, a father told his son to prepare the sled for a long journey. The day had arrived to take his own father out on the ice to die. He hooked the dogs to the sled and placed the aged grandfather upon it. He invited his son to come along.

Miles away, on the frozen tundra, he unhooked the sled and started to move away from the aged grandparent.

The son asked his father, "Why aren't we taking the sled?"

The father insisted it wasn't necessary.

But the son persisted, "We must, Father, we must. I will need it for you someday!"

Thankfully, we are no longer forced to abandon our elderly on some frozen tundra because they have lost their capacity to eat. Nevertheless, many aged parents are abandoned to rest in convalescent homes, forgotten by those who brought them there. There may be an occasional visit, but it's usually hurried and often seen more as a chore than as a time of sharing and intimacy!

If your grandparents are in a convalescent hospital or a retirement home, the next time you visit, *visit*. Spend some time really sharing and talking with your loved one. Don't be in a hurry to leave!

401 What Is the Cross?

Ask your grandparents to explain what they think is meant by the statement: "The cross is not an amulet, but an armor."

402 Build Relationships

We live in an age where individualism is emphasized more than relationships. Community—relationships—are secondary. Community is sharing and caring. It is what the early Christians discovered happened when they came into relationship with Christ Jesus at Pentecost:

> *They devoted themselves to the apostles' teaching and to the fellowship, to the breaking of bread and to prayer. Everyone was filled with awe, and many wonders and miraculous signs were done by the apostles. All the believers were together and had everything in common. Selling their possessions and goods, they gave to anyone as he had need. Every day they continued to meet in the temple courts. They broke bread in their homes and ate together with glad and sincere hearts, praising God and enjoying the favor of all the people.* Acts 2:42–47

When people are drawn into a relationship with Christ by the Holy Spirit, they are also drawn into relationship with one another. They care. They love one another. They think about more than just themselves. The Spirit enables them to show kindness, be sympathetic, forgive, share all things, and live together in gladness and joy.

This truth is represented by the cross itself. The Holy Spirit reaches down and draws us up to God through faith, represented by the vertical line of the cross. At the same time, He connects us with one another, represented by the horizontal line.

Draw a cross, and share this truth with your grandparents. Tell them you're happy that you're connected together as a family vertically and horizontally, and, because you are, you'll also be a family someday in heaven.

403 Why Do They Think So?

A. W. Tozer once said, "It is scarcely possible in most places to get anyone to attend a meeting where the only attraction is God." Ask your grandparents why they think that's the case.

404 A Tidbit about Age

Remind your grandparents of the following bit of wisdom: "We are all happier in many ways when we are old than when we were young. The young sow wild oats. The old grow sage."—Winston Churchill

"If You Were to Die Today"

St. Francis of Assisi was once asked, as he was hoeing his garden, "What would you do if you were suddenly to learn that you were to die at sunset today?" He replied, "I'd just keep on hoeing." Tell your grandparents what St. Francis said, and ask them how they'd answer the same question.

Repeating History

Someone once said, "Those who disregard the past are bound to repeat it." Ask your grandparents what part of the past they hope you'll remember so you don't repeat it.

Growth Means Life

Growth is essential; aging is inevitable. If you're not growing or aging, you're dead! Unfortunately, we deny that we are aging in whatever way we can and try to hide the evidence. Someone asks our age and we say, "Thirty-nine and holding." We get hair transplants to cover the balding. We buy "For Men Only" to cover up the graying beard! We get a "tummy tuck." We cut out our varicose veins via laser!

The next time your grandparents are lamenting their

protruding tummy or some other physical change that may be caused by aging, tell them these things are only a sign of growth, not aging!

Sobs, Sniffles, and Smiles

O. Henry once said, "Life is made up of sobs, sniffles, and smiles, with sniffles predominating." Ask your grandparents which of the three predominated in their lives.

Praise Them Openly

Someone once said, "Praise your children openly, reprove them secretly." One day my son heard his grandpa say to his neighbor, "I've got the smartest grandson in the world." My father didn't know Jacob heard him say it, but it made Jacob and me feel good. I thought, if he made Jacob feel so good with his good words about him, Grandpa would feel good if Jacob said good things about him. So one day Jacob told his friends that he thought he had the smartest grandpa in the whole wide world. Of course, he did it when he knew Grandpa was listening. It made Jacob feel good because when Grandpa turned around, he had a great big smile on his face.

Remember, "There are many ways to measure success; not the least of which is the way your child describes you when talking to a friend."

A Word for a Balding Grandpa

If your grandpa is balding, humor him with the following saying:

"Don't worry about losing hair; think of it as gaining face."—Unknown

A Visit to the Cemetery

Ask your grandparents to go through your local cemetery with you and tell you about any ancestors buried there.

Sayings and Their Meanings

Remind your grandparents of this saying: "You are today where your thoughts have brought you; you will be tomorrow where your thoughts take you." Ask them to give you their thoughts on the following sayings and to give examples in their life when they learned the truth of the proverb in one way or another.

a. "You'll never plow a field by turning it over in your mind."—Irish Proverb

b. "Every night I turn my worries over to God. He's going to be up all night anyway."—Mary C. Crowley

c. "We have a tendency to obscure the forest of simple joys with the trees of problems."—Christiane Collange

d. "And this, too, shall pass away."—Abraham Lincoln

e. "God grant me the sense of proportion to know the difference between an incident and a crisis."—Anonymous

f. "If you want to see God laugh, plan your life."—Anonymous

g. "Do what you can, with what you have, where you are."—Theodore Roosevelt

h. "Life is a short visit. So stop and smell the roses along the way."—Anonymous

413

Encouragement

When Elijah heard it, he pulled his cloak over his face and went out and stood at the mouth of the cave.

Then a voice said to him, "What are you doing here, Elijah?"

He replied, "I have been very zealous for the LORD God Almighty. The Israelites have rejected your covenant, broken down your altars, and put your prophets to death with the sword. I am the only one left, and now they are trying to kill me too."

The LORD said to him, "Go back the way you came, and go to the Desert of Damascus. When

you get there, anoint Hazael king over Aram …

So Elijah went from there. (1 Kings 19:13–15, 19)

When Elijah was feeling depressed, God told him to get up and start working, and he'd get over his discouragement.

Grandparents are like the rest of us! They can get discouraged at times. The next time your grandparents are discouraged, ask them to help you with a school project or some other task to help them get their minds off their worries.

Hope 414

It has long been known that there is a direct connection between the mind and the body. Recent medical studies have shown there is a direct correlation between a feeling of hopelessness and heart disease. For example, those who feel hopeless have a 20 percent greater chance of developing hardening of the arteries.

Make a conscious effort the next time you talk to your grandparents to tell them hopeful things such as:

"You're not old just because you're _____ years old. More and more people are reaching 80 years and above."

"Every birthday is a gift from God because each one makes you wiser!"

Ponder and Laugh

Humor honors a relationship. Write your grandparents a note and ask them what they think about the following statement:

"For God so loved the world that He gave His only begotten Son, that whosoever believeth in Him should not perish, but have ever-*laughing* life."

Laughter through a Funny Joke

Share some funny stories with your grandparents, such as the following:

You know what, Grandpa, Mom and I were driving home from school and an ambulance-like truck came rushing past us. It was some medical truck with a red cross printed on the side of it. It was obviously a carrier for some hospital. As it was rushing past us, an aluminum-like container fell out with a red cross printed on its side. It fell to the side of the road, and I knew the man in the truck didn't know it had fallen out because he just kept driving.

Mom quickly drove to the side of the road, and we jumped out of the car to see what was in the box. Inside the box was lots of ice and down in the center of the container was a large bottle with a large

179

toe floating in some fluid. It was even sort of bloody!

Obviously the toe was being transported from one hospital to another for someone who needed a toe. Can you imagine? (Build the suspense as much as you can.) Of course, we put it back into the ice, making sure it was covered, and put the lid back on the container.

(Wait for your grandpa to ask what you did next, then answer him.)

Well, what else could we do but call the "Toe Truck"?

(If he doesn't ask you what you did next, ask a question like, "I'll bet you must wonder what we did next, don't you, Grandpa?" Then, of course, be happy to tell him.)

Or tell the following story as if it were factual.

Grandpa, did you watch the news last night and hear about the young people who were dangling a mannequin on a long rope over the overpass and scaring the drivers below? After scaring the daylights out of quite a number of automobile drivers, a truck driver came along with a large hood on his truck. The news reporter said that the mannequin got caught on the hood of the truck. The boy had his arm swung around a pole on the overpass and so as the mannequin was grabbed by the truck, the boy's arm was literally jerked off his body.

The truck driver just kept driving, carrying the mannequin and arm down the highway. A highway patrol officer chased after the driver and arrested him.

(Play it up as best as possible, and hope that your grandpa will ask, "What did they arrest the truck driver for?")

For armed robbery, of course!

(If he doesn't ask, ask him if he knows what they arrested the truck driver for. Then tell him.)

Invite your grandparents to share with you a funny story as well. Why not agree to share one story a week, or, better yet, agree to make a journal of stories that might be kept as a family legacy!

Beliefs

One grandparent was asked the following question, "What do you believe about God?"

He answered, "I believe what my church teaches and believes."

"And what does your church teach and believe?"

"My church teaches and believes what I believe."

"What do you and your church believe?"

"Oh, we believe exactly the same thing."

Ask your grandparents what they believe about the following things:

1. Jesus
2. Sin
3. Forgiveness
4. Life eternal

418

When an Elderly Person Dies

Ask your grandparents to write down some of their thoughts about life that they hope will not disappear with their death.

419

Spread Your Wings

Challenge your grandparents to spread their wings academically and socially. When one continues to grow, one continues to stay alive.

The one thing we can continue to enjoy as we grow older is creativity. Invite your grandparents to be creative with you. For example, ask them to join you at the library and study about something you know nothing about (e.g., the progress of the electric car).

If your grandparents seem to have gotten into a rut, challenge them to visit a new place! Encourage them to go somewhere you've never been before and tell you all about it. Encourage them to redecorate. Or buy some new clothes. Or experience something new (e.g., going on a raft trip). Or challenge them to develop new interests (e.g., canning, garment weaving, giving massages).

Peer Pressure

A woman was asked what the best thing was about reaching age 102. She said, "No more peer pressure."

Ask your grandparents to help you with peer pressure.

What have they learned over the years about peers? How did they overcome peer pressure when they were younger? When did following the wrong kind of peer pressure get them in trouble? Why doesn't peer pressure matter as much to them now?

"How" and "Why"

The next time you talk to your grandparents or write them, use "how" and "why" questions rather than "what" or "who" questions.

"How did you manage to raise three children during the depression?"

"Why did you move to California?"

What Would the Title Be?

Ask your grandparents, if they wrote a book, what they would title it. Ask them to explain their title.

Accomplishments

Ask your grandparents about what accomplishments in life they are most proud.

The Story of Your Life

Ask your grandparents to write the story of their life in five short sentences.

When One Should Not Attempt Lying

Ask your grandparents in what ways over the years they've discovered this saying to be true: "Who is not sure of his memory, should not attempt lying."

Commitment

Ask your grandparents to tell you three to five things to which they are committed. Also tell them some of the things to which you are committed. Ask them what they think.

Stand for Something

Someone said, "Stand for something so you won't fall

for everything." Ask your grandparents what kinds of things they stood for over the years and what kinds of things they hope you will also stand for.

Who Has Been Your Coach?

Someone said, "Discipleship is playing for the coach and not the crowd." Ask your grandparents who has been their coach over the years. Ask them to explain.

President for a Day

Some people say there are two things people should never talk about: politics and religion. You should be able to talk to your grandparents about anything. Talk to them about their politics by asking the following question of them:

Do you know what man served as president of the United States for one day?

His name was David Rice Atchison and the year was 1849. The story of his presidency is as follows:

Zachary Taylor was the newly elected president. His inauguration was supposed to be on Sunday, as President James K. Polk officially concluded his duties on Saturday. Zachary requested to be sworn in with great pomp and circumstance on Monday. This meant someone needed to serve on Sunday. The President Pro Tem of the United Senate, David Atchison, was sworn in for one day! The story is that he was so exhausted from trying to finish all the business in

Congress from President Polk's last day, he fell asleep on Saturday evening and did not awaken until late on Sunday afternoon. This meant he missed his once-in-a-lifetime opportunity of making a difference as president of the United States.

Ask your grandparents: If you were president of the United States for a day, what would you do? What laws would you try to change? Which laws would you like to get passed? What kind of difference do you think you could make in a day?

Listen

Visit with your grandparents. As they talk, make a point to listen with your heart, not just your ears. Don't jump in with your point of view. Listen attentively with one goal in mind: to hear what they are saying.

Take a Risk

Taking risks isn't always easy; doing so takes us out of our comfort zone and increases the chance of failure. But doing so also opens us up to new experiences, new people, and new ways of doing things. Taking risks can enrich our lives in a way nothing else can.

Invite your grandparents to do something risky, such as going hot air ballooning or canoeing.

Cheering

During a political campaign in Illinois, organizers arranged for children to be excused from school to stand on the parade route and cheer, wave, and applaud as the vice president came by.

The children did as they had been instructed. They waved. They cheered. There was only one problem: The first motorcade that came by was a funeral.

Share this story with your grandparents. Tell them, as you see it, the cheering was appropriate if the person who had died was a Christian. That person would be in heaven! Quote Revelation 21:4: "He will wipe every tear from their eyes. There will be no more death or mourning or crying or pain for the old order of things has passed away." Ask them these questions:

- What do you think heaven will be like?
- What kinds of cheerful things do you want to happen at your funeral?
- Do you have any favorite songs you want sung? Favorite Bible verses to be read?

Additions to Webster's Dictionary

Each year new words are added to Webster's dictionary. Keep your grandparents informed by sharing with them some of the latest words you think may have been added over the last few years, such as: "Soccer mom"— 1) a mom who helps with her son's or daughter's soccer team, doing everything from making refreshments to refereeing; 2) a mom who spends most of her time driving her children from activity to activity. Ask which words they know of that have been added in their lifetime to the dictionary.

"How Are You Feeling?"

Ask your grandpa how he is feeling. When he tells you, listen to what he says. Don't minimalize it.

Past Hobby

Find out a past hobby or interest of your grandma (e.g., a sport, flower arranging). Do some research at the library or buy a book and study up on the subject. Then share the information with her. Ask her some questions about the hobby. Share what you learned about it.

"Choose Your Battles Wisely"

A wise uncle once said if you choose your battles wisely, you'll have more energy in winning those that are truly important. Some things matter; others don't!

Grandparents sometimes fear that young people don't want to hear what they have to say. Surprise them. Let them know you want to hear their wisdom. Request a block of time from them. Ask if you can sit down in some comfortable chairs in a quiet place away from the noise and hurry of everyday life. Tell them that you heard one should choose his or her battles wisely in life. Share that someone said if you choose your battles wisely, you'll be more effective in winning those that are important. Say to your grandparents:

- Tell me about some battles you've fought over the years (e.g., a battle over explosive anger).
- Which battles did you think were worth fighting? Describe some battles you think I shouldn't spend too much time fighting over, things that aren't that important in the whole scheme of things.
- Which battle do you think I should fight to the bitter end?

Credit Cards?

Most people today have credit cards. Most say that credit cards make it too easy to buy things on impulse. Ask your grandparents what their advice would be to you regarding credit cards.

"Tell Me a Story from Your Grandfather"

Ask your grandpa to tell you a story his grandpa told him.

The Stars

Go to your local library and check out a book on stars and the constellations. Invite your grandparents to join you some night in searching the skies to find specific stars or constellations.

On the Refrigerator Door

Write a special note of love and post it on your grandparents' refrigerator door.

Commercials and More Commercials

On the average, every American sees more than 1,800 commercial messages a day. Ask which ad is your grandma's favorite and why.

"Is It Really God's Word to Man?"

Ask your grandparents why they think some people who say the Bible is God's Word to man never read it.

Technology

Ask your grandparents what they think of all the new

advances in technology (i.e. the computer, cell phones, special medical procedures).

"Wherever You Go, There You Are"

Jon Kabat-Zinn wrote a book entitled, *Wherever You Go, There You Are* (New York, NY: Hyperion, 1995). Wherever you go, you take yourself. How many people do we hear say things like, "If only I could live over there, I'd be happy!" or "If I had a big home like so and so, I'd be happy too." For the most part, people don't change just because they live in a different area or live in a bigger home. They are who they are, wherever they are. People travel with their personalities, their habits, their peculiar characteristics. They don't leave them behind at the last place they were in. If you're a fun-loving person who likes to laugh a lot, you'll find that you're the same fun-loving person if you move thousands of miles away.

Ask your grandparents what they think. Do they agree, "Wherever you go, there you are"?

Praise Them

Experts tell us that a child needs four praises for every criticism to keep up his or her self-esteem. Grandparents need praise as well. Make a point to praise your grandparents with your words this week.

446

Two Killjoys

Charlie W. Shedd says that his grandfather taught him there are two ways to make oneself miserable: To say "If only" and to say "What if."

- "If only we hadn't moved from Minnesota."
- "If only I hadn't said what I said …!"
- "What if I can't pass the test?"
- "What if I have cancer?"

Shedd suggests: "Maybe my grandchildren need this word from me. Two certain killjoys: 'If only,' 'What if.' "[4]

Think about it! Maybe our grandparents need the same advice from us.

447

"Where Were You When?"

Ask your grandparents to tell you or to write down what they remember about when:

- The Japanese bombed Pearl Harbor on December 7, 1941.
- The United States dropped the Atomic Bomb on Hiroshima on August 6, 1945.
- John Kennedy was assassinated on November 22, 1963.
- Neil Armstrong walked on the moon on July 20, 1969.
- The Communist regime fell in the Fall of 1990.

A Special Telephone Call

Call your grandparents with no other purpose than to see how things are going. As they tell you, just love them and listen.

Live Now

Ralph Waldo Emerson said, "We are always getting ready to live but never living." Invite your grandparents to "live it up" with you by doing something they've never done before, such as going river rafting or sky diving.

A Pencil and a Question

Send your grandparents a lead pencil. Ask them to guess how long a line (in miles) the average pencil could draw before it ran out of lead. (The answer is approximately 35 miles.)

The Book of Proverbs

Make an agreement with your grandparents to read the book of Proverbs over the next 31 days—one chapter a day. After each one has read the chapter, discuss it via the telephone or in person.

If You Could Live It Over

Ask your grandparents to write down or share with you verbally how they would complete the phrase, "If I were to live my life over, I'd ..."

Memories Are a Part of Your Happiness

Ask your grandparents to share memories that are a part of their happiness with life. As they share them, listen attentively. You might even want to record them. You might not hear them again.

Forget One Thing in Life

Ask your grandparents, "If you could forget one thing about life, what would it be?"

A High School Yearbook

Ask your grandparents to show you their high school yearbooks. Tell them you'd like to see their pictures as well as pictures of their friends. Ask them to talk about their friends.

"Did God Make a Mistake?"

Ask your grandparents what they think of Mark Twain's statement: "Life would be infinitely happier if we could only be born at the age of eighty and gradually approach eighteen."

A Few Thoughts about Life and Death

Purchase a copy of *If I Should Die If I Should Live* by Joanne Markhausen (St. Louis, MO: Concordia Publishing House, 1975). Read the book together with your grandparents. It's a wonderful book for children and adults about life and death.

"Grandpa, How Far to School?"

Ask your grandpa how far he had to walk to school when he was a child. Then ask him if he thinks it's true that "The older a man gets, the farther he had to walk to school as a boy."

"Thanks for Such a Great Mother!"

Grandparents need to know that they did a good job of raising their children. Send them a note or tell them thank you for giving you such a great mother and father.

"Don'ts for Boys"

In my library of old books, I found one entitled *Don'ts for Boys* by Henry Altimus, published in 1902. Ask your grandparents if they remember any of these "don'ts" from when they were growing up. Talk about whether they still think these things are true today:

- "Don't introduce your acquaintances to girls unless you have permission and can vouch for their good character."
- "Don't neglect your bath. A robust boy should be an enthusiastic bather."
- "Be cheerful. Don't carry around a woebegone look or act as though all the trouble in the world were resting on your shoulders."

"Don'ts for Girls"

In my library I also found the book, *Don'ts for Girls* by Henry Altimus, published in 1903. Ask your grandparents if they remember any of the "don'ts" from when they were growing up. Talk about whether they still think these things are true today:

- "Don't consider it beneath you to know how to cook. It takes brains to master fine cookery."
- "Don't be ashamed of your parents. They may be unlearned and dull, but they gave you the chance to become what you are. Honor them before all men."

- "God made you for skirts. Don't dress like a man. Girls who do are as absurd as boys who are girlish. Never lose the sense of fitness."

It Makes Me Smile

Ask your grandparents to tell you some of the things that make them smile. When they're finished, share the things that make you smile. Compare your lists.

"Want" Not "Should"

There is a motto that says: "When you get older you can stop doing all the things you SHOULD do and start doing the things you WANT to do."

Ask your grandparents if they're following this motto. If not, why not?

Newspaper Clippings

Find newspaper stories that interest you and your grandparents. Send clippings to them and ask their opinion.

"What about Makeup?"

One survey says that 19 out of 20 American college women wear makeup. Ask your grandma if she wore makeup when she was growing up. Does she wear it now? What advice would she give you about wearing makeup? How much makeup is too much, too little?

"Who Was Your Favorite President?"

Ask your grandparents to tell you who their favorite president was and why.

Five Love Languages

Gary Chapman wrote a wonderful book entitled *The Five Love Languages*. He states that people share and receive love in different ways. He lists five "primary" expressions of love:

1. words of affirmation
2. quality time
3. receiving gifts
4. acts of service
5. physical touch[5]

Most people speak a primary love language. A grandma's primary love language might be number 5, physical touch, while her husband's is number 4, acts of service. A grandparent who is always making presents, wrapping them up, and giving them to others is saying that number 3, receiving gifts, is her primary love language. What every grandchild or child must learn to do is to speak whatever love language is primary for their grandparents. This may mean adopting a secondary love language that's different from the primary language.

Take time to read the book. When you do, analyze what your primary love language is and what you think your grandparents' love languages might be. Ask them to take the test to determine what their languages are. Once you've figured it out, figure out some ways you can love them with their primary love language.

468 Five Love Languages for Children

Invite your grandparents to better understand you and the other grandchildren by giving them a copy of the book *The Five Love Languages for Children* by Gary Chapman. It helps grandparents understand how their grandchildren express and receive love in different ways.

469 Words of Affirmation

One of the primary love languages Gary Chapman speaks of in his book, *The Five Love Languages*, is "words of affirmation." Resolve to speak this love language to your grandparents (compliment their neat yard, praise their appearance, mention how nice it was talking with them on the telephone).

Dead Plants

Erma Bombeck said one should never go to a doctor whose office plants have died. Ask your grandparents to check the plants out in the doctor's office the next time they go. Be sure to preface your request with what Erma Bombeck said.

1 Corinthians 13:4–8

Study St. Paul's words on love in 1 Corinthians 13.

Love is patient, love is kind. It does not envy, it does not boast, it is not proud. It is not rude, it is not self-seeking, it is not easily angered, it keeps no record of wrongs. Love does not delight in evil but rejoices with the truth. It always protects, always trusts, always hopes, always perseveres. Love never fails.

Underline those characteristics of love that you don't always practice with your grandparents. Then pray silently, asking God to help you put into practice more of these characteristics in the way you love others, especially your grandparents.

The End of a Conversation

End your next telephone conversation with your grandparents by saying, "I love you."

Share Their Favorite Verse

Ask your grandpa to share with you the one Scripture passage that he loves the most and that he'd like you to remember. Then write it down and do something special with it (e.g., write it in calligraphy, frame it, and present it to him as a picture).

Favorite Actor or Actress

Ask your grandparents who their favorite actor or actress was when they were teenagers. Then see if you can get a book on this actor or actress and give it to them. Or, see if your local video store has a video with the actor or actress starring in it. Rent it and watch it with your grandparents.

Get Rid of Worries

Invite your grandma to write down her worries on a sheet of paper. You do the same. Read together Matthew 6:25–34. Then tear up the sheets of paper and pray that you can forget your worries.

There Is No "Someday"

When your grandparents procrastinate doing important

things such as going to the doctor and say, "Someday I'll do it," lovingly remind them that "someday" is nowhere to be found in the week. Though there is "Mon-day," "Tues-day," "Wednes-day," etc., there is no "Some-day."

How to See a Rainbow

Typically, rainbows only appear after a rainstorm. Life is like that quite often as well: you have to put up with a lot of bad things before something good happens. Ask your grandparents to tell of a time when they had to "put up with the rain," but in the end saw "the rainbow."

God's Whisper in the Ear

Ask your grandpa, "Tonight, when you go to bed, if God would whisper one thing in your ear, what would you hope He would say to you?"

The First Kiss

Ask your grandma to describe her first kiss.

If There Were Only Three Books

Ask your grandparents, "If I could only read three books in my life, which three books would you hope they would be?"

"I'm So Proud to Have You as Grandparents"

Tell your grandparents, "I'm so proud you're my grandparents."

Thank Your Grandparents

What one physical feature have you inherited from your grandpa? The next time you see him, point out that distinctive feature, and thank him.

Quiz Time

Ask your grandparents at which age they think the average person hears best: 1) age 10; 2) age 24; 3) age 50; 4) age 72. (The answer is age 10.)

Getting Sick

Studies show that the average child gets sick three times a year. Ask your grandparents about times they remember getting sick as a child. What kind of medicine did their parents give them to help them get well?

"I'll Never Forget"

Tell your grandma when she loses her husband that you'll never forget grandpa. People who lose a spouse don't want others to forget the loved one!

An Inexpensive Way of Making Friends

There is a saying, "Politeness is an inexpensive way of making friends." Ask your grandparents to share with you some of the "musts" of being polite.

A Misquote

Ask your grandparents what they think happens to the person who believes the following: "The Lord is my shepherd, I can do what I want."

Fruit-Bearing Trees

"Stones and sticks are thrown only at fruit-bearing trees." Ask your grandparents why they think people throw stones "at fruit-bearing trees."

No Suggestions

Someone correctly said: "The Ten Commandments are not mere suggestions ..." Ask your grandparents what they think the Ten Commandments are.

Do More

The next time your grandparents ask you to do something, do more than is expected. Then ask them what they've discovered about work ethics over the years.

Religion That Costs

Ask your grandparents if they think "A religion that costs nothing does nothing." In what ways has their religion cost them over the years?

Which Words Have Been Most Helpful?

Ask your grandparents which words they have found

most helpful over the years (e.g., "thank you," "please").

Describe What "Love" Is

Ask your grandparents to describe "love" to you. What is it? How do I know when I'm "in love"?

Dying to Live

Ask your grandparents to explain what Dwight Moody meant when he said, "The Christian dies to live."

Do Ideas

Someone said, "Ideas are funny things, they do not work unless you do." Ask your grandparents to tell you about some ideas they had which they "did" and which paid off over the years.

Happiness?

Ask your grandparents to tell you what happiness is.

How to Break a Habit

Someone said, "One good way to break a bad habit: drop it." Ask your grandparents their advice on how to drop a bad habit.

"What Is a Friend?"

Ask your grandparents what they've learned over the years about friendship. Is it true that "the only way to have a friend is to be one"?

The Completion of a Picture

Draw half of a picture, then ask your grandpa to complete the other half.

Write It Down

Invite your grandparents to give their minds a break by writing down the important things they need to remember.

When They Are Having a Hard Time

When your grandparents are having an especially hard time with something, ask them to recall a pleasant memory with you (e.g., looking at an old photo album).

Endnotes

Section 1

1 Lee Meriwether, *Coming of Age Gracefully*, (Appleton, Wisconsin: Aid Association for Lutherans, 1995) p. 57.
2 E. Fritz Schmerl, *The Challenge of Age*, (New York, New York: Crossroads, 1991) p. 33.

Section 3

3 Ernest Thompson Seton, *Wild Animals at Home,* (Garden City, New York: Doubleday, Page & Company, 1913) p. 97.

Section 5

4 Charlie W. Shedd, *When God Created Grandparents and It Was Very Good,* (Garden City, New York: Doubleday & Company, Inc., 1976) pp. 64–65.
5 Gary Chapman, *The Five Love Languages*, (Chicago, Illinois: Northfield Publishing, 1992) p. 38.